Christmas Stories

By
Benjamin Leopold Farjeon

CHRISTMAS STORIES

STONEY-ALLEY.

In the heart of a very maze of courts and lanes Stoney-alley proclaims itself. It is one of multitude of deformed thoroughfares, which are huddled together--by whim, or caprice, or in mockery--in a populous part of the City, in utter defiance of all architectural rules. It is regarded as an incontrovertible law, that everything must have a beginning; and Stoney-alley could not have been an exception to this law. It is certain that the alley and its surrounding courts and lanes must once upon a time have been a space where houses were not; where, perhaps, trees grew, and grass, and flowers. But it is difficult to imagine; more difficult still to imagine how they were commenced, and by what gradual means one wretched thoroughfare was added to another, until they presented themselves to the world in the shapes and forms they now bear; resembling an ungainly body with numerous limbs, every one of which is twisted and deformed. Easier to fancy that they and all the life they bear sprang up suddenly and secretly one dark night, when Nature was in a sullen mood; and that being where they are, firmly rooted, they have remained, unchangeable and unchanging, from generation to generation. Records exist of fair islands rising from the sea, clothed with verdure and replete with animal fife; but this is the bright aspect of phenomena which are regarded as delusions by many sober persons. Putting imagination aside, therefore, as a thing of small account in these days (if only for the purpose of satisfying unbelievers), and coming to plain matter of fact, it is not to be doubted that Stoney-alley and its fellows grew upon earth's surface, and did sot spring up, ready-made, from below--although, truth to tell, it was worthy of such a creation. In the natural course of things, the neighbourhood must have had architects and builders; but no record of them is extant, and none is necessary for the purposes of this story. Sufficient that Stoney-alley rears its ugly body--though lowly withal--in the very heart of London, and that it may be seen any day in the week in its worst aspect. It has no other: it is always at its worst.

Out of it crawl, from sunrise until midnight, men and women, who, when they emerge into the wide thoroughfare which may be regarded as its parent, not uncommonly pause for a few moments, or shade their eyes with their hands, or look about them strangely, as if they have received a surprise, or as if the different world in which they find themselves requires consideration. Into it crawl, from sunrise until midnight, the same men and women, who, it may be observed, draw their breath more freely when they are away from the wide thoroughfares, and who plunge into Stoney-alley as dusty, heat-worn travellers might plunge into a refreshing bath, where the cool waters bring relief to the parched skin. What special comfort these men and women find there, would be matter for amazement to hundreds of thousands of other men and women whose ways of life, happily, lie in pleasanter places. But Stoney-alley, to these crawlers, is Home.

Its houses could never have been bright; its pavements and roads--for it has those, though rough specimens, like their treaders--could never have been fresh. Worn-out stones and bricks, having served their time elsewhere and been cashiered, were probably brought into requisition here to commence a new and unclean life. No cart had ever been seen in Stoney-alley: it was too narrow for one. A horse had once lived there--a spare sad blind horse belonging to a costermonger, who worked his patient servant sixteen hours a-day, and fed it upon Heaven knows what. It was a poor patient creature; and as it trudged along, with its head down, it seemed by its demeanour to express an understanding of its meanness. That it was blind may have been a merciful dispensation; for, inasmuch as we do not know for certain whether such beasts can draw comparisons as well as carts, it may have been spared the pangs of envy and bitterness, which it might have experienced at the sight of the well-fed horses that passed it on the road. It was as thin as a live horse well could be--so thin, that a cat might have been forgiven for looking at it with contempt, as being likely to serve no useful purpose after its worldly trudgings were ended. Its mane was the raggedest mane that ever was seen; and it had no tail. What of its hair had not been appropriated by its master the costermonger, had been plucked out ruthlessly, from time to time, by sundry boys and girls in Stoney-alley--being incited thereto by an ingenious youth, who plaited the horsehair into watchguards, and who paid his young thieves in weak liquorice-water, at the rate of a teaspoonful for every dozen hairs--long ones--from the unfortunate horse's tail. For years had this poor beast been wont to stumble over the stones in Stoney-alley when its day's work was over, and wait like a human being before its master's house for the door to open--rubbing its nose gently up and down the panels when a longer delay than usual occurred. The door being opened, it used to enter the narrow passage, and fill the house with thunderous sound as it walked into a little dirty yard, where a few charred boards (filched from a fire) had been tacked together in the form of a shed, which offered large hospitality to wind and rain. In this shed the wretched beast took its ease and enjoyed its leisure, and died one night so quietly and unexpectedly, that the costermonger, when he learnt the fact in the morning, cursed it for an ungrateful 'warmint,' and declared that if his dumb servant had yesterday shown any stronger symptoms of dying than it had usually exhibited, he would have sold it for 'two-pun-ten to Jimmy the Tinman.' So deeply was he impressed by the ingratitude of the animal, that he swore he would have nothing more to do with the breed; and he bought a donkey--a donkey with such a vicious temper, and such an obstinate disposition, that the costermonger, in his endeavours to render it submissive, became as fond of it as if it were one of his own kindred, and soon grew to treat it in exactly the same manner as he treated his wife. It would have been difficult, indeed, to decide which was the more important creature of the two--the wife or the donkey; for on two distinct occasions the costermonger was summoned before magistrate--once for ill-treating his wife, and once for ill-treating his donkey--and the sentence pronounced on each occasion was precisely the same. It may be noted as a curious contrast (affording no useful lesson that I am aware of), that when the costermonger came out of prison for ill-treating his wife, he went home and beat the poor creature unmercifully, who sat sobbing her heart out in a corner the while; and that when he came out of prison for ill-treating his donkey, he went into the rickety shed in his back-yard and belaboured the obstinate brute with a heavy stick. But the donkey, cunning after its kind, watched its opportunity, and gave the costermonger such a spiteful kick, that he walked lame for three months afterwards.

It would be unfair to the costermonger not to state, that he was not the only husband in those thoroughfares who was in the habit of beating his wife. He was but one of a very numerous Brute family, in whose breasts mercy finds no dwelling-place, and who marry and bring up children in their own form and likeness, morally as well as physically. It is to be lamented that, when the inhumanity of the members of this prolific family is brought before the majesty of the law for judgment--as is done every day of our lives--the punishment meted out is generally light and insignificant as compared to the offence. Yet it may be answered, that these wife-beaters and general Brutes were children once; and the question may be asked, Whether, taking into consideration that no opportunity was offered to them of acquiring a knowledge of a better condition of things, they are fully responsible for their actions now that they are men? We wage war against savage beasts for our own protection. But how about savage men, who might have been taught better--who might have been humanised? We press our thumb upon them, and make laws to punish the exercise of their lawless passions. But have they no case against us? Is all the right on our side, and all the wrong on theirs? That the problem is an old one, is the more to be lamented; every year, nay, every hour, its roots are striking deeper and deeper into the social stratum. The proverb, 'when things are quiet, let them be quiet,' is a bad proverb, like many others which are accepted as wisdom's essence. Not by a man's quiet face, but by his busy brain and heart, do we judge him. If there be benevolence in statesmanship, the problem should be considered in its entirety, without delay. By and by it may be too late.

PART I.

A STRANGE EVENT OCCURS IN STONEY-ALLEY.

Delicate feather-flakes of snow were floating gently down over all the City. In some parts the snow fell white and pure, and so remained for many hours. In other parts, no sooner did it reach the ground than it was converted into slush--losing its purity, and becoming instantly defiled. This was its fate in Stoney-alley; yet even there, as it rested upon the roofs and eaves, it was fresh and beautiful for a time. In which contrasted aspects a possible suggestion might arise of the capability of certain things for grace and holiness, if they are not trodden into the mire.

An event had just occurred in Stoney-alley which was the occasion of much excitement. This was nothing more or less than the birth of twin-girls in one of the meanest houses in the alley. The mother, a poor sickly woman, whose husband had deserted her, was so weakened and prostrated by her confinement, and by the want of nourishing food, that she lived but a dozen days after the birth of her babes. No one knew where the father was; he and his wife had not lived long in the neighbourhood, and what was known of him was not to his credit, although with a certain class he was not unpopular. He was lazy, surly fellow, who passed his waking hours in snarling at the better condition of things by which he was surrounded. The sight of carriage made his blood boil with envy; notwithstanding which he took delight in walking in the better thoroughfares of the City, and feeding his soul with the bitter sight of well-dressed people and smiling faces. Then he would come back to his proper home, and snarl at society to pot-house audiences, and in his own humble room would make his unhappy wife unhappier by his reviling and discontent He called himself working-man, but had as much right to the title as the vagabond-beggar who, dressed in broadcloth, is wheeled about in an easy-chair, in the West-end of London, and who (keeping a sharp look-out for the police the while) exhibits placard proclaiming himself to be a respectable commercial traveller, who has lost the use of his limbs. He traded upon the title, however, and made some little money out of it, hoping by and by to make more, when he had become sufficiently notorious as a public agitator. In the mean time, he (perhaps out of revenge upon society) deserted his wife when she was near her confinement, and left her to the mercy of strangers. She could not very well have fared worse than she did in that tender charge. She bore two babes, and died without a sign.

The mother was buried the day before Christmas, and the babes were left to chance charity. There were many women lodgers in the house in which the twin-girls had been born; but not one of them was rich enough to take upon herself the encumbrance of two such serious responsibilities. The station-house was spoken of, the Foundling, the workhouse; but not a soul was daring enough to carry out one of the suggestions. This arose from a fear of consequences--in the shape perhaps of an acknowledged personal responsibility, which might prove troublesome in the event of the station-house, the workhouse, or the Foundling refusing to take charge of the infants. Moses in the bulrushes was not in a worse plight than these unfortunate babes in Stoney-alley.

What on earth was to be done with them? Every person in the house might get into trouble, if they were left to die. The house, small as it was, accommodated five or six distinct families--each occupying room--in addition to two bachelors--one a vagrant, the other hawker in cheap glassware. These last could not be expected to assume the slightest shadow of responsibility. At length, a bright idea struck a charitable woman in the house. Armed only with calico apron with a large bib and an immense pocket in front (like stomacher), the charitable soul went about to solicit contributions in aid of the infants. As she walked round and about the narrow alleys and courts, soliciting from everybody, she made quite a stir in the neighbourhood by the vigorous manner in which she rattled the coppers in her capacious pocket. A great many gave, farthings and halfpence being in the ascendant--the largest contribution being given by the bachelor vagrant above mentioned, who gave twopence with the air of a gentleman--better still, with the true spirit of one; for he gave more than he could afford, and took no glory to himself for the action. Attracted by the rattle of the coppers, a singular-looking little man, with a shrivelled face, came to the door of his shop, and was instantly accosted by the kindhearted soul.

'You'll give a copper or two, I know, Mr. Virtue,' said the woman.

'Then you know more than I do,' replied the man. 'I don't give. I lend.'

'What'll you lend on 'em, then?' asked the woman good-humouredly.

'Lend on what?'

'On the poor little twins that was born in our house a fortnight ago?'

'O, that's what you're up to,' exclaimed the man, whose eyes were the most extraordinary pair that ever were seen in human face--for one was as mild as London milk, and the other glared like fury. 'That's what you're up to. Collectin' for them brats afore they learn to tell lies for theirselves.'

'They're as sweet a pair as ever you see,' said the woman. 'Just give it a thought, Mr. Virtue; you're a man o' sense----'

'Yah!' from the man, in the most contemptuous of tones, and with the fiercest of glares from his furious eye.

'There they are, without mother, as 'elpless as 'elpless can be,' persisted the woman, with wonderful display of cheerfulness. 'Come, now, you'll give a copper although you do look so grumpy.'

The cynic turned into his dark shop at this last appeal, but as he turned a penny dropped from his pocket. The woman picked it up with a pleasant laugh, and adding it to her store proceeded on her charitable mission. But industrious and assiduous as she was, the sum-total collected was very small; about sufficient to keep the infants for half a week. The kindhearted woman took the babes, and nursed them pro tem. She had a family of dirty children of her own, who were bringing themselves up in the gutters; for she could not attend to them, so fully was her time occupied in other ways. She could not, therefore, be expected to take permanent charge of the motherless babes. And so her husband told her, grumblingly, when he came home from his work on Christmas-eve. All that she said was, 'Poor little things!' and fell to--rough as she was--detecting imaginary beauties in the babies' faces--a common trick of mothers, which no man can afford to be cross with, especially in his own wife, and the woman who has borne him children.

'Can't put 'em out in the cold, the pretty dears!' said the woman tenderly.

'We've got enough of our own,' responded her husband not unkindly, and yet with a certain firmness; 'and there's more coming--worse luck!' But these last two words he said beneath his breath, and his wife did not hear them.

'All the more reason for being kind to these,' said the woman. 'They'll be handsome girls when they grow up. Look'ee here, Sam, this one's got a dimple, just like--like----' Her voice trailed off softly, and her husband knew that she was thinking of their first-born, that had lived but a few weeks.

I am aware that it is the fashion with a large class to regard the portrayal of sentiment among very common people as fanciful and untrue to nature. I differ from this class, I am glad to say. True love for women, and true tenderness for children, are common to all of us, whether high or low. Cynics cannot alter what is natural--in others.

The man felt kindly towards his wife and the babes, but he was not at all inclined to saddle himself with a couple of ready-made infants. He saw, however, that his wife was in a foolishly tender mood, and he let the subject drop for the present.

It may have been eight o'clock in the white night, and the bright snow was still falling like feathers from angels' wings, when at the door of the house in which the twins had been born and the mother had died, a lady and gentleman stopped, and, obtaining entrance, asked for the landlady. Unmistakably lady and gentleman, though plainly dressed. Not highly born, but as truly lady and gentleman as the best in the land. They were strangers to the landlady of the house; but she rose the instant they entered her apartment, and remained standing during the interview.

'We have to apologise for this intrusion,' commenced the lady, in a gentle voice; 'but although we are strangers to you, we are not here out of rudeness.'

'I'm sure of that, ma'am,' replied the landlady, dusting two chairs with her apron. 'Will you and the gentleman take a seat?'

'This is my husband,' said the lady, seating herself. 'Every year, on the anniversary of this evening, with the exception of last year, we have been in the habit of coming to some such place as this, where only poor people live----'

'Ah, you may say that, ma'am! The poorest!'

----'It is so, unfortunately. God help them! Every year until the last we have been in the habit of coming to some such place in furtherance of a scheme--a whim, perhaps, you'll call it--the development of which gives us the chief pleasure of our lives. We have no family of our own, no children that can properly call me mother and my husband father; so every year we adopt one and bring it up. We have six now, as many as we have been able to keep; for last year we lost part of our means through unwise speculation, for which I and my husband were equally to blame----'

'I'm sorry to hear that, ma'am,' interposed the landlady sympathisingly, standing in an attentive attitude, with the corner of her apron between her fingers.

'And having as many little responsibilities on us as our means would enable us to take proper care of, we were unable to add another to our family of little ones. But this year a fortunate thing has occurred to us. A kind friend has placed a small sum at our disposal, which will enable us to take a seventh child, and rear it in comfort and respectability.'

'And a lucky child that seventh 'ull be,' remarked the landlady. 'I'm a seventh child myself, and so was my mother before me, and we was both born on a th.'

The lady smiled, and continued,

'Every child we have is an orphan, without father or mother, which we believe to be necessary for the proper furtherance of our scheme. We feed them and nourish them properly--indeed, as if they were really our own--and when they are old enough, they will be put to some respectable occupation, which will render them independent of the world. Among the many poor children round about here, do you know of one who, having no natural protectors, would be bettered by coming under our charge? These letters will satisfy you of our fitness for the task, and that we are in earnest.'

'Lord bless me!' exclaimed the landlady, impelled to that exclamation by sudden thought of the twins upstairs, and not casting a glance at the papers which were placed in her hands. 'You don't mean what you say?'

'Indeed, we do. You will be kind enough to understand that we do not desire to take a child who has parents living, but one whom hard circumstance has placed in the world friendless and alone. These poor courts and alleys abound in children----'

'Ah, that they do; and a nice pest they are, a many on 'em. They're as thick as fleas.'

----'And at this season it is good to think of them, and to try to do some little thing in their behalf. It is but little that we can do--very, very little. Do you know of such a child as we seek for now?'

'A girl?

'A girl or boy.'

'God Almighty bless you, ma'am!' cried the landlady. 'Stop here minute, and I'll let you know.'

She ran in haste upstairs to where her kind-hearted lodger was nursing the twins.

'I beg you a thousand pardons, Mrs. Manning,' she said, panting, 'and you too, Mr. Manning, and I wish you a merry Christmas, and many on 'em! I'm that out of breath and that astonished, that I don't know if I'm on my head or my heels. Stay a minute, my good souls; I'll be back in a jiffey.'

With that, she ran out of the room and downstairs, to assure herself that her visitors had not flown, or that she had not been dreaming. Having satisfied herself she ran upstairs again, and sat down, in more panting state than before.

'I thought I was dreaming, and that they was apparitions.' she gasped.

Mr. Manning, being one of those Englishmen who look upon their habitations as their castles, was inclined to resent these intrusions. Unconsciously throwing a large amount of aggressiveness in his tone and manner, he asked his landlady if he owed her any rent, and received for answer, No, that he didn't, and the expression of a wish that everybody was like him in this respect.

'Very well, then,' said Mr. Manning, not at all mollified by the landlady's compliment, and speaking so surlily that (as the landlady afterwards said, in relating the circumstance) if it had not been for her being out of breath and for thinking of those two precious babes, he would have 'put her back up' there and then; 'if I don't owe you anything, what do you mean by coming bouncing into my room in this manner?'

'I asks your pardon,' said the landlady, with dignity; but instantly softening as she thought of her visitors down-stairs; 'but you've got a 'art in your bosom, and you've got the feelings of a father. The long and the short of it is'----and here she proceeded to explain the visit she had had, and the object of her visitors. 'Ah, Mr. Manning,' she continued, following the direction of his eyes towards the two babes lying in his wife's lap, 'you've got the same idea as I had in coming up here. Here's these two blessed babes, with no mother, and no father to speak of; for I don't believe he'll ever turn up. What's to become of 'em? Who's to take care of 'em? I'm sure you can't.'

'No, that I can't; and don't intend to.'

'And no one expects you, sir. You've got a big-enough family of your own. Well, here's this lady and gentleman setting downstairs this blessed minute as wants a child, and as'll do what's right and proper by it.'

'But there's a pair of 'em. Won't they take the two?'

'One they said, and one they mean. They can't hardly afford that, they said. And I'm as certain as I am that I'm setting here, that if they knew there was two of 'em, they wouldn't part 'em for the world. No, they'd go somewhere else; and the chance 'd be lost.'

'But they want a child that ain't got no father nor mother. Now, these young uns have a father; and that you know.'

'No, I don't; I don't know nothing of the kind. 'Taint the first story I've told by a many,' said the landlady, in answer to Mr. Manning's look of astonishment; 'and I don't mind telling this one to do a little baby good.'

'What's to become of the other? 'We'll look after her between us.

One'll take her one day, and one another. Lord bless you, Mr. Manning, we shall be able to manage.'

'And if the father comes back?'

'I'll get the lady's address, and give it to him; and then he can do as he likes.'

'It's the best thing that can be done; said Mr. Manning; 'though I've nothing to do with it, mind you; it's none of my business. I've got troubles enough of my own. But it ain't every young un that gets such a chance.'

'No, that it ain't;' and the landlady pulled her chair close to that of Mrs. Manning. 'Which shall it be, my dear?'

This proved to be a very difficult question to answer. First they decided that it was to be this one, then that; then soft-hearted Mrs. Manning began to cry, and said it was a sin to part them. And the babes lay sleeping unconsciously the while this momentous point was being discussed, the decision of which might condemn one to want and dirt and misery--to crime perhaps--and the other to a career where good opportunity might produce a happy and virtuous life. At length it was decided, and one was chosen; but when the landlady prepared to take the child, she found that the fingers of the babes were tightly interlaced; so she left them in Mrs. Manning's lap, with instructions to get the chosen one ready, and went down to her visitors.

'Poor child!' said the lady, at the conclusion of the landlady's recital; 'and the mother was only buried yesterday!'

'Only yesterday, ma'am,' responded the landlady; 'and the dear little thing is left without a friend. There's not one of us that wouldn't be glad to take care of it; but we're too poor, ma'am; and that's the fact.'

'The child's younger than we could have wished,' mused the lady, with a glance at her husband; 'but it would seem like a cruel desertion, now that we have heard its sad story.'

Her husband nodded, and the landlady, keenly watchful, said eagerly:

'I'll bring it down to you, ma'am. One of the lodgers is nursing it; but her husband's grumbling at her, and making her miserable about it He says he's got enough of his own; and so he has.'

By this time Mrs. Manning had the baby ready--she had dressed the child in some old baby-clothes of her own--and before she let it go out of her arms, she said, as if the little thing could understand:

'Kiss sister, baby. You'll never see her again, perhaps; and if you do, you won't know her.'

She placed their lips close together; and at that moment they opened their eyes, and smiled prettily on one another. The man and the two women stood by, gazing earnestly at the babes. Tears were in Mrs. Manning's eyes, as she witnessed the strange parting; the landlady was silent and pensive; and the man, with his hands behind him, seemed to be suddenly engrossed in the consideration of some social problem, which he found too perplexing for him. His wife raised the fortunate babe to his face.

'A happy New-year to you, little un,' said the not unkindly man, as he kissed the child.

'Suppose they were our'n, Sam,' said his wife, softly and tearfully; 'we shouldn't like this to happen.'

'But they're not our'n,' replied her husband; 'and that makes all the difference.'

And yet there was a wistful expression on his face, as the landlady took the baby out of the room.

'I've kept the prettiest one,' his wife whispered to him--'the one with the dimple.'

The lady and gentleman--she with her new charge wrapped in her warm shawl, and pressed closely to her bosom--walked briskly through the cold air towards their home, which lay in a square, about a mile from Stoney-alley. In the centre of the square was a garden, the wood-growth in which, though bare of leaves, looked as beautiful in their white mantle as ever they had done in their brightest summer. The snow-lined trees stood out boldly, yet gracefully, and their every branch, fringed in purest white, was an emblem of loveliness. They gleamed grandly in the moon's light, mute witnesses of the greatness of Him whose lightest work is an evidence of perfect wisdom and goodness.

HOW SHE ACQUIRED THE NAME OF BLADE-O'-GRASS.

Thus, whilst one little babe was tended and watched by benevolent hands and eyes, the fate of the other--the prettier one, she with the unfortunate dimple--was intrusted to the shapeless hands of chance. To such tender care as had happily fallen to its lot, the fortunate one may be left for a time. Turn we to the other, and watch its strange bringing-up.

Proverbially, too many cooks spoil the broth; and this forlorn babe was left to the care of too many cooks, who, however, in this instance, did not spoil the broth by meddling with it, but by almost utterly neglecting it. The landlady's declaration that 'We'll look after her between us; one'll take her one day, and one another,' although uttered in all sincerity, turned out badly in its application. What is everybody's business is nobody's business, and for the most part the babe was left to take care of herself. For a little while Mrs. Manning was the child's only friend; but in the course of a couple of months she fulfilled her husband's apprehension, and added another bantling to his already overstocked quiver. This new arrival (which, it must be confessed, was not received with gratitude by its father) was so fractious, and so besieged by a complication of infantile disorders, that all Mrs. Manning's spare moments were fully occupied, and she had none to devote to other people's children. The motherless child threatened to fare badly indeed. But now and again a mother who had lost her offspring came to the little stranger and suckled her; so that she drew life from many bosoms, and may be said to have had at least a score of wet-nurses. And thus she grew up almost literally in the gutters, no one owning her, no one really caring for her; and yet she throve, as weeds thrive--while her sister, not a mile away, throve, in the care of kind friends, as flowers thrive. Born in equality, with the same instincts for good and evil, with the same capacity for good and evil, equally likely to turn out good or bad, should it have been left entirely to chance that one might live to prove a blessing, and the other a curse, to society? But so it was.

One of the most curious circumstances connected with the little outcast was, that she was not known by any settled name. It grew to be a fashion to call her by all sorts of names--now Polly, now Sally, now Young Hussy, now Little Slut, and by a dozen others, not one of which remained to her for any length of time. But when she was three years of age, an event occurred which played the part of godmothers and godfathers to her, and which caused her to receive a title by which she was always afterwards known.

There was not a garden in Stoney-alley. Not within the memory of living man had a flower been known to bloom there. There were many poor patches of ground, crowded as the neighbourhood was, which might have been devoted to the cultivation of a few bright petals; but they were allowed to lie fallow, festering in the sun. Thought of graceful form and colour had never found expression there. Strange, therefore, that one year, when Summer was treading close upon the heel of Spring, sending warm sweet winds to herald her coming, there should spring up, in one of the dirtiest of all the backyards in Stoney-alley, two or three Blades of Grass. How they came there, was a mystery. No human hand was accountable for their presence. It may be that a bird, flying over the place, had mercifully dropped a seed; or that a kind wind had borne it to the spot. But however they came, there they were, these Blades of Grass, peeping up from the ground shyly and wonderingly, and giving promise of bright colour, even in the midst of the unwholesome surroundings. Our little castaway--she was no better--now three years of age, was sprawling in this dirty backyard with a few other children, all of them regular students of Dirt College. Attracted by the little bit of colour, she crawled to the spot where it shone in the light, and straightway fell to watching it and inhaling, quite unconsciously, whatever of grace it possessed. Once or twice she touched the tender blades, and seemed to be pleased to find them soft and pliant. The other children, delighted at having the monopoly of a gutter, that ran through the yard, did not disturb her; and so she remained during the day, watching and wondering; and fell asleep by the side of the Blades of Grass, and dreamed perhaps of brighter colours and more graceful forms than had ever yet found place in her young imagination. The next day she made her way again to the spot, and seeing that the blades had grown a little, wondered and wondered, and unconsciously exercised that innate sense of worship of the beautiful which is implanted in every nature, and which causes the merest babes to rejoice at light, and shapes of beauty, and harmony of sound. What is more wonderful, in the eyes of a babe, than vivid colour or light, however kindled? what more sweet to its senses than that perfect harmony of sound which falls upon its ears as the mother sings softly and lulls her darling to sleep? This latter blessing had never fallen to the lot of our child; but colour and light were given to her, and she was grateful for them. She grew to love these emerald leaves, and watched them day after day, until the women round about observed and commented upon her strange infatuation. But one evening, when the leaves were at their brightest and strongest, a man, running hastily through the yard, crushed the blades of grass beneath his heel, and tore them from the earth. The grief of the child was intense. She cast a passionate yet bewildered look at the man, and picking up the torn soiled blades, put them in the breast of her ragged frock, in the belief that warmth would bring them back to life. She went to bed with the mangled leaves in her hot hand, and when she looked at them the next morning, they bore no resemblance to the bright leaves which had been such a delight to her. She went to the spot where they had grown, and cried without knowing why; and the man who had destroyed the leaves happening to pass at the time, she struck at him with her little fists. He pushed her aside rather roughly with his foot, and Mrs. Manning, seeing this, and having also seen the destruction of the leaves, and the child's worship of them, blew him up for his unkindness. He merely laughed, and said he wouldn't have done it if he had looked where he was going, and that it was a good job for the child that she wasn't a Blade-o'-Grass herself, or she might have been trodden down with the others. The story got about the alley, and one and another, at first in fun or derision, began to call the child Little Blade-o'-Grass, until, in course of time, it came to be recognised as her regular name, and she was known by it all over the neighbourhood. So, being thus strangely christened, Little Blade-o'-Grass grew in years and in ignorance, and became a worthy member of Dirt College, in which school she was matriculated for the battle of life.

THE LEGEND OF THE TIGER.

At a very early age indeed was Blade-o'-Grass compelled to begin the battle of life. Her greatest misfortune was that, as she grew in years, she grew strong. Had she been a weakly little thing, some one might have taken pity on her, and assumed the responsibility of maintaining her. The contingency was a remote one; but all chance of benefiting by it was utterly destroyed, because she was strong and hardy. She may be said to have had some sort of a home up to the time that she attained the age of nine years; for a corner for her to sleep in was always found in the house in which she was born. But about that time certain important changes took place, which materially affected her, although she had no hand in them. The landlady gave up the house, and some one else took it, and turned it into a shop. The lodgers all received notice to leave, and went elsewhere to live. A great slice of luck fell to the share of Mr. Manning. An uncle whom he had never seen died in a distant land, and left his money to his relatives; and a shrewd lawyer made good pickings by hunting up nephews and nieces of the deceased. Among the rest, he hunted up Mr. Manning, and one day he handed his client a small sum of money. Mr. Manning put his suddenly acquired wealth to a good purpose--he got passage in a government emigrant ship, and with his wife and large family, bade good-bye for ever to Stoney-alley. He left the country, as hundreds and thousands of others have done, with a bitter feeling in his heart because he was not able to stop in it, and earn a decent livelihood; but, as hundreds and thousands of others have done, he lived this feeling down, and in his new home, with better prospects and better surroundings, talked of his native land--meaning Stoney-alley--as the 'old country,' in terms of affection and as if he had been treated well in it. It will be easily understood that when Blade-o'-Grass lost Mrs. Manning, she lost her best friend.

To say that she passed an easy life up to this point of her career would be to state what is false. The child was in continual disgrace, and scarcely a day passed that was not watered with her tears. Blows, smacks, and harsh words were administered to her freely, until she grew accustomed to them, and they lost their moral force. She deserved them, for she was the very reverse of a good little girl. In a great measure her necessities made her what she was, and no counteracting influence for good approached her. If she were sent for beer, she would stop at corners, and taste and sip, and bring home short measure. There was something fearful in her enjoyment; but she had no power nor desire to resist the temptation. No tragedy queen, before the consummation of the final horror, ever looked round with more watchful, wary, fearsome gaze than did Blade-o'-Grass, when, having nerved her soul to take a sip of beer, she stopped at a convenient corner, or in the shadow of a dark doorway, to put her desire into execution. And then she was always breaking things. The mugs she let fall would have paved Stoney-alley. But there was a greater temptation than beer: Bread. If she were sent for a half-quartern loaf, she would not fail to dig out with liberal fingers the soft portions between the crusts, and eagerly devour them. Even if she had not been hungry--which would have been a white-letter day in her existence--she would have done from habit what she almost invariably was urged to do by the cravings of her stomach. And about that unfortunate stomach of hers, calumnies were circulated and believed in. So persistent an eater was Blade-o'-Grass, so conscientious a devourer of anything that, legitimately or otherwise, came in her way--quality being not of the slightest object--that a story got about that she had 'something' in her inside, some living creature of a ravenous nature, that waited for the food as she swallowed it, and instantly devoured it for its own sustenance. Such things had been known of. At some remote period a girl in the neighbourhood--whose personality was never traced, but whom everybody believed in--had had such an animal--a few called it a 'wolf,' but the majority insisted that it was a 'tiger'--growing inside of her, and this animal, so the story went, grew and grew, and fed upon the girl's life till it killed her. The 'tiger' had been found alive after the girl's death, and having been purchased of some one for a fabulous price, was embalmed in a bottle in a great museum, of which nobody knew the name or the whereabouts. As an allegory, this 'tiger' might have served to illustrate the mournful story of the lives of Blade-o'-Grass and thousands of her comrades--it might have served, indeed, to point a bitter moral; but there was nothing allegorical about the inhabitants of Stoney-alley. They only dealt in hard matter-of-fact, and the mythical story was fully believed in; and being applied to the case of Blade-o'-Grass, became a great terror to her. Many persons found delight in tormenting the helpless child about her 'tiger,' and for a long time the slightest allusion to it was sufficient to cause her the most exquisite anguish, in consequence of certain malevolent declarations, that she ought to be cut open and have the tiger taken out of her. Indeed, one miserable old fellow, who kept a rag-shop, and who had in his window two or three dust-coated bottles containing common-place reptiles preserved in spirits-of-wine, took a malicious pleasure in declaring that the operation ought to be really performed upon Blade-o'-Grass, and that, in the interests of science, she ought not to be allowed to live. It was the cruelest of sport thus to torture the poor child; for the simple fact was, that Blade-o'-Grass was nearly always hungry. It was nature tugging at her stomach--not a tiger.

The very first night of Mrs. Manning's departure, Blade-o'-Grass found herself without a bed. With a weary wretched sense of desolation upon her, she lingered about the old spot where she used to sleep, and even ventured to enter at the back of the house, when the sharp 'Come, get out o' this!' of the new proprietor sent her flying away. She belonged to nobody, and nobody cared for her; so she wandered and lingered about until all the lights in the shops and houses were out. She had gleaned some small pleasure in watching these lights; she had found comfort in them; and when they were all extinguished and she was in darkness, she trembled under the impulse of a vague terror. She did not cry; it was not often now that she called upon the well of tender feeling where tears lay; but she was terrified. There was not a star in the sky to comfort her. She was in deep darkness, body and soul. How many others are there at this present moment in the same terrible condition?

Too full of fear to stand upright, she crept along the ground slowly, feeling her way by the walls, stopping every now and then to gather fresh courage, at which time she tried to shut out her fears by cowering close to the flagstones and hiding her face in her ragged frock. She had a purpose in view. She had thought of a refuge where she would find some relief from the terrible shadows. Towards that refuge she was creeping now. It was a long, long time before she reached her haven--a crazy old lamp-post, the dim light of which was in keeping with the general poverty of its surroundings. At the foot of this lamp-post, clasping it as if it were the symbol of a sacred refuge, Blade-o'-Grass looked up at the light in agony of speechless gratitude, and then, wearied almost to a state of unconsciousness, coiled herself up into a ball, like a hedgehog, and soon was fast asleep.

THE BATTLE OF LIFE.

What followed? Remorseless Time pursued his way, and the minutes, light to some, heavy to some, leaving in their track a train of woe and joy, and grief and happiness; the leaden minutes, the golden minutes, flew by until daylight came and woke the sleeping child. Unwashed--but that was her chronic condition, and did not affect her--forlorn, uncared-for, Blade-o'-Grass looked round upon her world, and rubbed her eyes, and yawned; then, after a time, rose to her feet, and cast quick eager glances about her. The tiger in her stomach was awake and stirring, and Blade-o'-Grass had no food to give it to satisfy its cravings. She prowled up and down, and round and about the dirty courts, in search of something to eat; anything would have more than contented her--mouldy crust, refuse food; but the stones of Stoney-alley and its fellows were merciless, and no manna fell from heaven to bless the famished child. She would have puzzled the wisest philosopher in social problems, if he were not utterly blinded by theory; for, looking at her from every aspect, and taking into account, not only that she was endowed with mental, moral, and physical faculties, but that she was a human being with a soul 'to be saved,' he could have produced but one result from her--a yearning for food. He could have struck no other kind of fire from out of this piece of flint. What resemblance did Blade-o'-Grass bear to that poetical image which declared her to be noble in reason, infinite in faculty, express and admirable in form and bearing; like an angel in action; like a god in apprehension? The beauty of the world! the paragon of animals! Perhaps it will be best for us not to examine too curiously, for there is shame in the picture of this child-girl prowling about for food. Poor Blade-o'-Grass! with every minute the tiger in her stomach grew more rabid, and tore at her vitals tigerishly. In the afternoon she found a rotten apple in the gutter, and she stooped and picked it up, joy glistening in her eyes. It was a large apple, fortunately, and she devoured it eagerly, and afterwards chewed the stalk. That was all the food she got that day; and when night came, and she had watched the lights out, she coiled herself up into a ball by the side of her lamp-post again and slept, and awoke in the morning, sick with craving. Yesterday's experience whispered to her not to look about for food in Stoney-alley; and she walked, with painful steps into the wider thoroughfare, and stopped for a few minutes to recover herself from her astonishment at the vast world in which she found herself. She would have been content to stop there all the day, but that the tiger cried for food, and she cried for food in sympathy with the tiger. Keeping her eyes fixed upon the ground, and never once raising her pitiful face to the faces that flashed past her, hither and thither, she faltered onwards for a hundred yards or so, and then, in a frightened manner, retraced her steps, so that she should not lose herself. 'Give me food!' cried the tiger, and 'Give me food!' cried Blade-o'-Grass from the innermost depths of her soul. At about ten o'clock in the morning, her cry was answered; she saw a cats'-meat man with a basket full of skewered meat hanging upon his arm. Instinctively she followed him, and watched the cats running to the doors at the sound of his voice, and waiting with arched backs and dilating eyes for his approach. Blade-o'-Grass wished with all her heart and soul that she were a cat, so that she might receive her portion upon a skewer; but no such happiness was hers. She followed the man wistfully and hungeringly, until he stopped at the door of a house where there were evidently arrears of account to be settled. He placed his basket upon the doorstep, and went into the passage to give some change to the woman of the house. Here was an opportunity for Blade-o'-Grass. She crept stealthily and fearfully towards the basket, and snatching up two portions of cats'-meat, ran for her life, with her stolen food hidden in her tattered frock--ran until she reached Stoney-alley, where she sank to the ground with her heart leaping at her throat, and where, after recovering her breath, she devoured her ill-gotten meat with unbounded satisfaction. She had no idea that she had done a wrong thing. She was hungry, and had simply taken food when the opportunity presented itself. The fear by which she had been impressed had not sprung from any moral sense, but partly from the thought that the man would hurt her if he caught her taking his property, and partly from the thought (more agonising than the other) that she might be prevented from carrying out her design. The next day she watched for and followed the cats'-meat man again, and again was successful in obtaining a meal; and so on for a day or two afterwards. But the food was not over nice, and the tiger whispered to her that a change would be agreeable. Success made her bold, and she looked about her for other prey. Her first venture, after the cats'-meat man lost her patronage, was an old woman who kept an apple-stall, and who went to sleep as regularly as clockwork every afternoon at three o'clock and woke at five. But even in her sleep this old apple-woman seemed to be wary, and now and then would mumble out with drowsy energy, 'Ah, would yer? I sees yer!' as if the knowledge that she was surrounded by suspicious characters whose mouths watered for her fruit had eaten into her soul. But as these exclamations to terrify poachers were mumbled out when the old woman really was in an unconscious state, she fell an easy victim to Blade-o'-Grass. She was a great treasure to the little girl, for she dealt in nuts and oranges as well as apples. Then there was a woman who sold a kind of cake designated 'jumbles,'--a wonderful luxury, price four a penny. She also fell a victim, and between one and another Blade-o'-Grass managed to pick up a precarious living, and in a few months became as nimble and expert a little thief as the sharpest policeman would wish to make an example of. She was found out, of course, sometimes, and was cuffed and beaten; but she was never given in charge. The persons from whom she stole seemed to be aware of the hapless condition of the child, and had mercy upon her; indeed, many of them had at one time or another of their lives known what it was to suffer the pangs of hunger.

Incredible as it may sound, Blade-o'-Grass still had one friend left. His name was Tom Beadle. He was some five years older than Blade-o'-Grass, but looked so delicate and sickly, and was of such small proportions, that they might have been taken for pretty nearly the same age. Delicate and sickly as he looked, he was as sharp as a weasel. He had a mother and a father, who, when they were not in prison, lived in Stoney-alley, but they--being a drunken and dissolute pair--did not trouble themselves about their son. So he had to shift for himself, and in course of time became cunningest of the cunning. Between him and Blade-o'-Grass there had grown a closer intimacy than she had contracted with any other of her associates, and whenever they met they stopped to have a chat Blade-o'-Grass had a genuine affection for him, for he had often given her a copper, and quite as often had shared his meal with her.

A few months after the change for the worse in the prospects of Blade-o'-Grass, Tom Beadle, lounging about in an idle humour, saw her sitting on the kerb-stone with her eyes fixed upon the old apple-woman, who had begun to nod. There was something in the gaze of Blade-o'-Grass that attracted Tom Beadle's attention, and he set himself to watch. Presently the girl shifted a little nearer to the fruit-stall--a little nearer--nearer, until she was quite close. Her hand stole slowly towards the fruit, and a pear was taken, then another. Tom Beadle laughed; but looked serious immediately afterwards, for Blade-o'-Grass was running away as fast as her legs could carry her. Assuring himself that there was no cause for alarm, Tom Beadle ran after her, and placed his hand heavily on her shoulder. She had heard the step behind her, and her heart almost leaped out of her throat; but when she felt the hand upon her shoulder, she threw away the stolen fruit, and fell to the ground in an agony of fear.

'Git up, you little fool,' exclaimed Tom Beadle. 'What are you frightened at?' Before he said this, however, he picked up the pears and put them in his pocket.

'O, Tom!' cried Blade-o'-Grass, the familiar tones falling upon her ears like sweetest music; 'I thought it was somebody after me.'

Then Tom told her that he ran after her to stop her running, and instructed her that it was the very worst of policy, after she had 'prigged' anything, to run away when nobody was looking. And this was the first practical lesson in morals that Blade-o'-Grass had received.

'But, I say, Bladergrass,' observed Tom, 'I didn't know as you'd taken to prig.'

'I can't help it, Tom. The tiger's always at me.'

Tom implicitly believed in the tiger story.

'Well, that's all right,' said Tom; 'only take care--and don't you run away agin when nobody's a-lookin'.'

Months passed, and Blade-o'-Grass lived literally from hand to mouth. But times grew very dull; her hunting-ground was nearly worked out, and she was more often hungry than not. One day she hadn't been able to pick up a morsel of food, and had had insufficient for many previous days. The day before she had had but one scanty meal, so that it is not difficult to imagine her miserable condition. Her guardian angel, Tom Beadle, discovered her crouching against a wall, with fear and despair in her face and eyes. He knew well enough what was the matter, but he asked her for form's sake, and she returned him the usual answer, while the large tears rolled down her cheeks into her mouth.

It so happened that Tom Beadle had been out of luck that day. He hadn't a copper in his pocket. He felt about for one, nevertheless, and finding none, whistled--curiously enough, the 'Rogues' March'--more in perplexity than from surprise.

'Ain't yer had anythink to eat, Bladergrass?'

'Not a blessed bite,' was the answer.

It was about five o'clock in the evening; there were at least a couple of hours to sunset. An inspiration fell upon Tom Beadle, and his countenance brightened.

'Come along o' me,' he said.

Blade-o'-Grass placed her hand unhesitatingly in his, and they walked towards the wealthier part of the City, until they came to a large space surrounded by great stone buildings. In the centre of the space was a statue. Blade-o'-Grass had never been so far from her native place as this. The crowds of people hurrying hither and thither, as if a moment's hesitation would produce, a fatal result; the apparently interminable strings of carts and cabs and wagons and omnibuses issuing from half-a-dozen thoroughfares, and so filling the roads with moving lines and curves and angles, that it seemed to be nothing less than miraculous how a general and disastrous crash was avoided, utterly bewildered little Blade-o'-Grass, and caused her for a moment to be oblivious of the cravings of the tiger in her stomach.

'Now, look 'ere, Bladergrass,' whispered Tom Beadle: 'you keep tight 'old of my 'and; if anybody arks yer, I'm yer brother a-dyin' of consumption. I'm a-dyin' by inches, I am.'

Forthwith he called into his face such an expression of utter, helpless woe and misery, that Blade-o'-Grass cried out in terror,

'O, what's up, Tom? O, don't, Tom, don't!' really believing that her companion had been suddenly stricken.

'Don't be stoopid!' remonstrated Tom, smiling at her to reassure her, and then resuming his wobegone expression; 'I'm only a-shammin'.'

With that he sank upon the bottom of a grand flight of stone steps, dragging Blade-o'-Grass down beside him. There they remained, silent, for a few moments, and perhaps one in a hundred of the eager bustling throng turned to give the strange pair a second glance; but before sympathy had time to assume practical expression, a policeman came up to them, and bade them move on. Tom rose to his feet, wearily and painfully, and slowly moved away: a snail in its last minutes of life could scarcely have moved more slowly, if it had moved at all. He took good care to keep tight hold of the hand of Blade-o'-Grass, lest she should be pushed from him and be lost in the crowd. A notable contrast were these two outcasts--she, notwithstanding her fright and the pangs of hunger by which she was tormented, strong-limbed and sturdy for her age; and he drooping, tottering, with a death-look upon his face, as if every moment would be his last. You would have supposed that his mind was a blank to all but despair, and that he was praying for death; but the cunning and hypocrisy of Tom Beadle were not to be measured by an ordinary standard. He was as wide awake as a weasel, and although his eyes were to the ground, he saw everything that surged around him, and was as ready to take advantage of an opportunity as the sharpest rascal in London. As he and his companion made their way through the busy throng, they attracted the attention of two men--both of them elderly men, of some sixty years of age; one, well-dressed, with a bright eye and a benevolent face; the other, poorly but not shabbily dressed, and with a face out of which every drop of the milk of human kindness seemed to have been squeezed when he was a young man. When he looked at you, it appeared as if you were undergoing the scrutiny of two men; for one of his eyes had a dreadfully fixed and glassy stare in it, and the other might have been on fire, it was so fiercely watchful.

Now, overpowered as Tom Beadle might have been supposed to be in his own special ills and cares, he saw both these men, as he saw everything else about him, and a sly gleam of recognition passed from his eyes to the face of the odd-looking and poorly-dressed stranger; it met with no response, however. The next moment Tom raised his white imploring face to that of the better-dressed man, whose tender heart was stirred by pity at the mute appeal. He put his hand in his pocket, but seemed to be restrained from giving; some impulse within him whispered, 'Don't!' while his heart prompted him to give. But the struggle was not of long duration. The words, 'Indiscriminate charity again,' fell from his lips, and looking round cautiously as if he were about to commit a felony, he hastily approached close to the two children, and, with an air of guilt, slipped a shilling in Tom Beadle's hand. After which desperate deed, he turned to fly from the spot, when he saw something in the face of the odd-looking man (who had been watching the comedy with curious interest) which made him first doubtful, then angry. Although they were strangers, he was impelled to speak, and his kind nature made him speak in a polite tone.

'Dreadful sight, sir, dreadful sight,' he said, pointing to the creeping forms of Tom Beadle and Blade-o'-Grass. 'A penny can't be thrown away there, eh?'

The odd-looking man shrugged his shoulders. The shrug conveyed to the benevolent stranger this meaning: 'You are an imbecile; you are an old fool; you are not fit to be trusted alone.' It was the most expressive of shrugs.

'I suppose you mean to say I've been imposed upon,' exclaimed the benevolent stranger hotly.

The odd-looking man chuckled enjoyably, and perked up his head at the questioner in curiosity, as a magpie with its eye in a blaze might have done. But he said nothing. His silence exasperated the benevolent almsgiver, who exclaimed, 'You've no humanity, sir; no humanity;' and turned on his heel. But turned round again immediately and said, 'I've no right to say that, sir--no right, and I beg your pardon. But d'ye mean to tell me that that lad is an impostor, sir? If you do, I deny it, sir, I deny it! D'ye mean to say that I've been taken in, and that those two children are not--not HUNGRY, sir?'

Some words seemed to be rising to the odd-looking man's lips, but he restrained the utterance of them, and closed his lips with a snap. He touched his shabby cap with an air of amusement, and turned away, chuckling quietly; and the next minute the two men were struggling in different directions with the human tide that spread itself over all the City.

In the mean time, Tom Beadle, keeping up the fiction of 'dyin' by inches,' crept slowly away. He had not seen the coin which had been slipped into his hand, but he knew well enough by the feel that it was a shilling. 'A regular slice o' luck,' he muttered to himself, beneath his breath. When they had crept on some fifty yards, he quickened his steps, and Blade-o'-Grass tried to keep up with him. But all at once her hands grew quite cold, and a strong trembling took possession of her.

'Come along, Bladergrass,' urged Tom, in his anxiety to get safely away; "ow you creep!'

The child made another effort, but, as if by magic, the streets and the roar in them vanished from her sight and hearing, and she would have fallen to the ground, but for Tom's arm thrown promptly round her poor fainting form.

Near to them was a quiet court--so still and peaceful that it might have hidden in a country-place where Nature was queen--and Tom Beadle, who knew every inch of the ground, bore her thither. His heart grew cold as he gazed upon her white face.

'I wish I may die,' he muttered to himself, in a troubled voice, 'if she don't look as if she was dead. Bladergrass! Bladergrass!' he called.'

She did not answer him. Not a soul was near them. Had it not been that he liked the child, and that, little villain as he was, he had some humanity in him--for her at least--he would have run away. He stood quiet for a few moments, debating within himself what he had best do. He knelt over her, and put his lips to hers, and whispered coaxingly, 'Come along, Bladergrass. Don't be a little fool. Open your eyes, and call Tom.'

The warmth of his face and lips restored her to consciousness. She murmured, 'Don't--don't! Let me be!'

'What's the matter, Bladergrass?' he whispered. 'It's me--Tom! Don't you know me?'

'O, let me be, Tom!' implored Blade-o'-Grass. 'Let me be! The tiger's a-eatin' the inside out o' me, and I'm a-dyin'.'

She closed her eyes again, and the sense of infinite peace that stole upon her, as she lay in this quiet court, was like heaven to her, after the wild roar of steps and sounds in which a little while since she had been engulfed. Had she died at that moment, it would have been happier for her; but at whose door could her death have been laid?

Tom Beadle, whispering hurriedly and anxiously, and certainly quite superfluously, 'Lay still, Bladergrass! I'll be back in a minute,' ran off to buy food, and soon returned with it. He had a little difficulty in rousing her, but when she began to taste the food, and, opening her eyes, saw the store which Tom had brought, she tore at it almost deliriously, crying out of thankfulness, as she ate. Tom was sufficiently rewarded by seeing the colour return to her cheeks; before long, Blade-o'-Grass was herself again, and was laughing with Tom.

'But I thought you was a-dyin', Bladergrass,' said Tom, somewhat solemnly, in the midst of the merriment.

'No, it was you that was a-dyin', Tom!' exclaimed Blade-o'-Grass, clapping her hands. 'A-dyin' by inches, you know!'

Gratified vanity gleamed in Tom Beadle's eyes, and when Blade-o'-Grass added, 'But, O Tom, how you frightened me at first!' his triumph was complete, and he enjoyed an artist's sweetest pleasure. Then he gloated over the imposition he had practised upon the benevolent stranger, and cried in glee,

'Wasn't he green, Bladergrass? He thought I was dyin' by inches, as well as you. O, O, O!' and laughed and danced, to the admiration of Blade-o'-Grass, without feeling a particle of gratitude for the benevolent instinct which had saved his companion from starvation.

After this fashion did Blade-o'-Grass learn life's lessons, and learn to fight its battles. Deprived of wholesome teaching and wholesome example; believing, from very necessity, that bad was good; without any knowledge of God and His infinite goodness, she, almost a baby-child, went out into the world, in obedience to the law of nature, in search of food. A slice of bread-and-butter was more to her than all the virtues, the exercise of which, as we are taught, bestows the light of eternal happiness. And yet, if earnest men are to be believed, and if there be truth in newspaper columns, the vast machinery around her was quick with sympathy for her, as one of a class whom it is man's duty to lift from the dust. Such struggles for the amelioration (fine word!) of the human race were being made by earnest natures, that it was among the most awful mysteries of the time, how Blade-o'-Grass was allowed to grow up in the ignorance which deprives crime of responsibility; how she was forced to be dead to the knowledge of virtue; how she was compelled to earn the condemnation of men, and to make sorrowful the heart of the Supreme!

MR. MERRYWHISTLE RELIEVES HIMSELF ON THE SUBJECT OF INDISCRIMINATE CHARITY.

The name of the man who gave Tom Beadle the shilling was Merrywhistle. He was a bachelor, and he lived in the eastern part of the City, in Buttercup-square, next door to his best friends, the Silvers. Although Buttercup-square was in the east of the City, where the greatest poverty is to be found, and where people crowd upon each other unhealthfully, it was as pretty and comfortable a square as could be found anywhere; and you might live in any house in it and fancy yourself in the country, when you looked out of window. The trees in the square were full of birds' nests, and the singing of the birds of a summer morning was very sweet to the ear.

Mr. Merrywhistle had no trade or profession. When the last census was taken, and the paper was given to him to fill-in, he set himself down as 'Nothing Particular,' and this eccentric definition of himself coming under the eyes of his landlady--who, like every other landlady, was mighty curious about the age, religion, and occupation of her lodgers, and whether they were single, widowed, or divorced men--was retailed by her to her friends. As a necessary consequence, her friends retailed the information to their friends; and for some little time afterwards, they used to ask of the landlady and of each other, jocosely, how Nothing Particular was getting along, and whether he had lately done Anything Particular; and so on. But this mildest of jokes soon died out, and never reached Mr. Merrywhistle's ears. He had an income more than sufficient for his personal wants; but at the year's end not a shilling remained of his year's income. A pale face, a look of distress, a poor woman with a baby in arms, a person looking hungrily in a cook-shop window--any one of these sights was sufficient to melt his benevolent heart, and to draw copper or silver from his pocket. It was said of him that his hands were always in his pockets--a saying which was the occasion of a piece of sarcasm, which grew into a kind of proverb. A lady-resident of Buttercup-square, whose husband was of the parsimonious breed, when speaking of Mr. Merrywhistle's benevolence, said, with a sigh, 'My husband is just like Mr. Merrywhistle; his hands are always in his pockets.' 'Yes, ma'am,' said an ill-natured friend, 'but there the similarity ends. Your husband's hands never come out.' Which produced a lifelong breach between the parties.

Mr. Merrywhistle was in a very disturbed mood this evening. He was haunted by the face of the old man who had been amused, because he had given a poor child, a shilling. The thought of this old man proved the most obstinate of tenants to Mr. Merrywhistle; having got into his mind, it refused to be dislodged. He had never seen this man before, and here, in the most unaccountable manner, he being haunted and distressed by a face which presented itself to his imagination with a mocking expression upon it, because he had been guilty of a charitable act. 'I should like to meet him again,' said Mr.

Merrywhistle to himself; 'I'd talk to him!' Which mild determination, hotly expressed, was intended to convey an exceedingly severe meaning. As he could not dislodge the thought of the man from his mind, Mr. Merrywhistle resolved to go to his friends next door, the Silvers, and take tea with them. He went in, and found them, as he expected, just sitting down to tea. Only two of them, husband and wife.

'I am glad you have come in,' said Mrs. Silver to him. Her voice might surely have suggested her name, it was so mild and gentle. But everything about her was the same. Her dress, her quiet manner, her delicate face, her hands, her eyes, where purity dwelt, breathed peace and goodness. She and her sisters (and there are many, thank God!) are the human pearls of the world which is so often called 'erring.'

'How are the youngsters?' asked Mr. Merrywhistle, stirring his tea.

'All well,' answered Mr. Silver; 'you'll stay and see them?'

Mr. Merrywhistle nodded, and proceeded with his tea. The meal being nearly over, Mrs. Silver said, 'Now, friend, tell us your trouble.'

'You see it in my face,' responded Mr. Merrywhistle.

'Yes; I saw it when you entered.'

'You have the gift of divination.'

'Say, the gift of sympathy for those I love.'

Mr. Merrywhistle held out his hand, and she grasped it cordially. Then he told them of the occurrence that took place on the Royal Exchange, and of the singular manner in which he was haunted by the mocking face of the old man who had watched him.

'You have an instinct, perhaps,' said Mrs. Silver, 'that he was one of the men who might have preached at you, if he had had the opportunity, against indiscriminate charity?'

'No, I don't know, I don't know, I really don't know,' replied Mr. Merrywhistle excitedly. 'I think he rather enjoyed it; he seemed to look upon it as an amusing exhibition, for he was almost convulsed by laughter. Laughter! It wasn't laughter. It was a series of demoniac chuckles, that's what it was--demoniac chuckles. But I can't exactly describe what it was that set my blood boiling. It wasn't his demoniac chuckling alone, it was everything about him; his manner, his expression, his extraordinary eyes; one of which looked like the eye of an infuriated bull, as if it were half inclined to fly out of its head at you, and the other as if it were the rightful property of the meekest and mildest of baa-lambs. Then his eye-brows--lapping over as if they were precipices, and as thick as blacking-brushes. Then his face, like a little sour and withered apple. Your pro-indiscriminate-charity men would not have behaved as he did. They would have asked me. How dare I--how dare I?--yes, that is what they would have said--How dare I encourage pauperism by giving money to little boys and girls and ragged men and women, whom I have never seen in my life before, whom I have never heard of in my life before? This fellow wasn't one of them. No, no--no, I say, he wasn't one of them. I wouldn't swear that he wasn't drunk--no, I won't say that; tipsy, perhaps--no, nor that either. Uncharitable of me--very. Don't laugh at me. You wouldn't have laughed at the poor little boy if you had seen him.'

'I am sure we should not.'

'That's like me again,' cried the impetuous old bachelor remorsefully; 'throwing in the teeth of my best friends an accusation of inhumanity--yes, inhumanity--positive inhumanity. Forgive me--I am truly sorry. But that indiscriminate-charity question cropped up again to-day, and that, as well as this affair, has set my nerves in a jingle. A gentleman called upon me this morning, and asked me for a subscription towards the funds of an institution--a worthy institution, as I believe. I hadn't much to spare--I am so selfishly extravagant that my purse is always low--and I gave him half-a-sovereign. He took it, and looked at it and at me reproachfully. "I was given to understand," he said in the meekest of voices, so meek, indeed, that I could hot possibly take offence--"I was given to understand that from Mr. Merrywhistle, and in aid of such an institution as ours, I should have received a much larger contribution."'

'That savoured of impertinence,' observed Mr. Silver.

'I daresay, Silver, I daresay. Another man might have thought so; but I couldn't possibly be angry with him, his manner was so humble--reproachfully humble. I explained to him that at present I couldn't afford more, and that, somehow or other, my money melted away most surprisingly. "I hope, sir," he then said, "that what I was told of you is not true, and that you are not in the habit of giving away money indiscriminately." I could not deny it--no, indeed, I could not deny it--and I commenced to say, hesitatingly (feeling very guilty), that now and then---- But he interrupted me with, "Now and then, sir!--now and then! You will pardon my saying so, Mr. Merrywhistle, but it may not have struck you before that those persons who give away money indiscriminately are making criminals for us--are filling our prisons--are blowing a cold blast on manly self-endeavour--are crippling industry--are paying premiums to idleness, which is the offspring of the----hem!" And continued in this strain for more than five minutes. When he went away, my hair stood on end, and I felt as if sentence ought to be pronounced upon me at once. And here, this very afternoon, am I caught again by a pitiful face--you should have seen it! I thought the poor boy would have died as I looked at him--and I give away a shilling, indiscriminately. Then comes this strange old fellow staring at me--sneering at me, shrugging his shoulders at me, and walking away with the unmistakable declaration--though he didn't declare it in words--that I wasn't fit to be trusted alone. As perhaps I'm not,--as perhaps I'm not!' And Mr. Merrywhistle blew his nose violently.

His friends knew him too well to interrupt him. The tea-things had been quietly cleared away, while he was relieving his feelings. He had by this time got rid of a great portion of his excitement; and now, in his cooler mood, he looked round and smiled. At that moment a lad of about fifteen years of age entered the room. All their countenances brightened, as also did his, as he entered.

'Well, Charley,' said Mr. Merrywhistle, as the lad, with frank face, stood before him, 'been knocking anything into "pie" to-day?'

'No, sir,' replied Charley. 'I'm past that now; I'm getting along handsomely, the overseer said.'

'That's right, my boy; that's right. You'll be overseer yourself, some day.'

Charley blushed; his ambition had not yet reached that height of desire, and it seemed almost presumption to him to look so far ahead. The overseer in the printing-office where Charley was apprenticed was a great man in Charley's eyes; his word was law to fifty men and boys. The lad turned to Mr. Silver, and said in a pleased tone:

'A new apprentice came in today, and swept out the office instead of me.'

'So you are no longer knight of the broom?

'No, sir, and I'm not sorry for it; and there's something else. Dick Trueman, you know, sir--'

'You told us, Charley; he was out of his time last week, and they gave him a frame as a regular journeyman.'

'Yes, sir; and he earnt thirty-four shillings last week--full wages. And what do you think he did today, sir?' And Charley's bright eyes sparkled more brightly. These small items of office-news were of vast importance to Charley--almost as important as veritable history. 'But you couldn't guess,' he continued, in an eager tone. 'He asked for three hours' holiday--from eleven till two--and he went out and got married!'

'Bless my soul!' exclaimed Mr. Merrywhistle, 'he can't be much more than twenty-one years of age.'

'Only a few weeks more, sir. But he's a man now. Well, he came back at two o'clock, in a new suit of clothes, and a flower in his coat. All the men knew, directly they saw him, that he had asked for the three hours' holiday to get married in. And they set up such a clattering--rattling on their cases with their sticks, and on the stone with the mallets and planers--that you couldn't hear your own voice for five minutes; for every one of us likes Dick Trueman. You should have seen Dick blush, when he heard the salute! He tried to make them believe that he didn't know what all the clattering was about. But they kept it up so long, that he was obliged to come to the stone and bob his head at us. It makes me laugh only to think of it. And then the overseer shook hands with him, and Dick sent for three cans of beer, and all the men drank his health and good luck to him.' Charley paused to take breath. The simple story, as he told it in his eager way, was a pleasant story to hear. Now came the most important part of it Charley's eyes grew larger as he said, with much importance, 'I saw her.'

'Who?' they asked.

'Dick's wife; she was waiting at the corner of the street for him--and O, she's Beautiful!'

'Quite a day of excitement, Charley,' said Mr. Silver.

'There's something more, sir.'

'What is it, Charley?'

'Our wayz-goose comes off next week, sir.'

'Yes, Charley.'

'Only two of the apprentices are asked, and I'm one of them,' said Charley, with a ring of pardonable pride in his voice. 'May I go?

'Certainly, my boy,' said Mr. Silver. And Mrs. Silver smiled approvingly, and told Charley to run and wash himself and have tea; and Charley gave them all a bright look, and went out of the room as happy a boy as any in all London.

Then said Mr. Merrywhistle:

'Charley's a good lad.'

'He's our first and eldest,' said Mrs. Silver, bringing forward a basket filled with socks and stockings wanting repair; 'he will be a bright man.'

Mr. Merrywhistle nodded, and they talked of various subjects until the sound of children's happy voices interrupted them. 'Here are our youngsters,' he said, rubbing his hands joyously; and as he spoke a troop of children came into the room.

MRS. SILVER'S HOME.

There were five of them, as follows:

The eldest, Charles, the printer's apprentice, fifteen years of age--with a good honest face and a bright manner. The picture of a happy boy.

Then Mary, fourteen years. She looked older than Charley, and, young as she was, seemed to have assumed a kind of matronship over the younger branches. That the position was a pleasing one to her and all of them was evident by the trustful looks that passed between them.

Then Richard, twelve years; with dancing eyes, open mouth, and quick, impetuous, sparkling manner--filled with electricity--never still for a moment together; hands, eyes, and every limb imbued with restlessness.

Then Rachel, eleven years; with pale face and eyes--so strangely watchful of every sound, that it might almost have been supposed she listened with them. She was blind, and unless her attention were aroused, stood like a statue waiting for the spark of life.

Lastly, Ruth. A full-faced, round-eyed child, the prettiest of the group. Slightly wilful, but of a most affectionate disposition.

Rachel inclined her head.

'There's some one here,' she said.

'Who, my dear?' asked Mrs. Silver, holding up a warning finger to Mr. Merrywhistle, so that he should not speak.

Rachel heard his light breathing.

'Mr. Merrywhistle,' she said, and went near to him. He kissed her, and she went back to her station by the side of Ruth.

They were a pleasant bunch of human flowers to gaze at, and so Mr. and Mrs. Silver and Mr. Merrywhistle thought, for their eyes glistened at the healthful sight. Ruth and Rachel stood hand in hand, and it was easily to be seen that they were necessary to each other. But pleasant as the children were to the sight, a stranger would have been struck with amazement at their unlikeness to one another. Brothers and sisters they surely could not be, although their presence there and their bearing to each other betokened no less close a relationship. They were not indeed related by blood, neither to one another, nor to Mr. and Mrs. Silver. They were Mrs. Silver's foundlings--children of her love, whom she had taken, one by one, to rear as her own, whom she had snatched from the lap of Destitution.

Her marriage was one of purest affection, but she was barren; and after a time, no children coming, she felt a want in her home. Her husband was secretary in a sound assurance office, and they possessed means to rear a family. Before their marriage, they had both dwelt in thought upon the delight and pure pleasure in store for them, and after their marriage she saw baby-faces in her dreams. She mused: 'My husband's son will be a good man, like his father, and we shall train him well, and he will be a pride to us.' And he: 'In my baby daughter I shall see my wife from her infancy, and I shall watch her grow to girlhood, to pure womanhood, and shall take delight in her, for that she is ours, the offspring of our love.' But these were dreams. No children came; and his wife still dreamt of her shadow-baby, and yearned to clasp it to her bosom. Years went on--they had married when they were young--and her yearning was unsatisfied. Pain entered into her life; a dull envy tormented her, when she thought of homes made happy by children's prattle, and her tears flowed easily at the sight of children. Her husband, engrossed all the day in the duties and anxieties of his business, had less time to brood over the deprivation, although he mourned it in his leisure hours; but she, being always at home, and having no stern labour to divert her thoughts from the sad channel in which they seemed quite naturally to run, mourned with so intense a grief, that it took possession of her soul and threatened to make her life utterly unhappy. One day he awoke to this, and quietly watched her; saw the wistful looks she cast about her, unaware that she was being observed; felt tears flowing from her eyes at night. He questioned her, and learnt that her grief and disappointment were eating into her heart; that, strive as she would, her life was unhappy in its loneliness while he was away, and that the sweetest light of home was wanting.

'I see baby-faces in my dreams,' she said to him one night, 'and hear baby-voices--so sweet, O, so sweet!' She pressed him in her arms, and laid his head upon her breast. 'And when I wake, I grieve.'

'Dear love,' he said, all the tenderness of his nature going out in his words, 'God wills it so.'

'I know, I know, my love,' she answered, her tears still flowing.

'How can I fill up the void in her life?' he thought, and gave expression to his thought.

Then she reproached herself, and asked his forgiveness, and cried, in remorse, 'How could she, how could she grieve him with her sorrow?'

'I have a right to it,' he answered. 'It is not all yours, my dear. Promise me, you in whom all my life's cares and joys are bound, never to conceal another of your griefs from me.'

She promised, and was somewhat comforted. This was within a couple of months of Christmas. A few nights before Christmas, as he was walking home, having been detained later than usual at his office, he came upon a throng of people talking eagerly with one another, and crowding round something that was hidden from his sight. It was bitterly cold, and the snow lay deep. He knew that nothing of less import than a human cause could have drawn that concourse together, and could have kept them bound together on such a night, and while the snow was falling heavily. He pushed his way through the crowd to the front, and saw a policeman gazing stupidly upon two forms lying on the ground. One was a man--dead; the other a baby--alive in the dead man's arms. He had them--the living and the dead--conveyed to the station-house; inquiries were set afoot; an inquest was held. Nothing was learnt of the man; no one knew anything of him; no one remembered having ever seen him before; and the mystery of his life was sealed by his death. He told his wife the sad story, and kept her informed of the progress, or rather the non-progress, of the inquiry. The man was buried, and was forgotten by all but the Silvers. Only one person attended the parish funeral as mourner, and that was Mr. Silver, who was urged to the act by a feeling of humanity.

'The poor baby? said Mrs. Silver, when he came from the funeral--'what will become of it?'

In the middle of the night she told her husband that she had dreamt of the baby. 'It stretched out its little arms to me.'

Her husband made no reply; but a few nights afterwards, having arranged with the parish authorities, he brought home the child, and placed it in his wife's arms. Her heart warmed to it immediately. A new delight took possession of her; the maternal instinct, though not fully satisfied, was brought into play. During the evening she said, 'How many helpless orphans are there round about us, and we are childless!' And then again, looking up tenderly from the babe in her lap to her husband's face, 'Perhaps this is the reason why God has given us no children.'

From this incident sprang the idea of helping the helpless; and year after year an orphan child was adopted, until they had six, when their means were lessened, and they found they could take no more. Then Mr. Merrywhistle stepped in, and gave sufficient to lift another babe from Desolation's lap. This last was twin-sister to Blade-o'-Grass, and they named her Ruth. From this brief record we pass to the present evening, when all the children are assembled in Mrs. Silver's house in Buttercup-square.

Some little time is spent in merry chat--much questioning of the children by Mr. Merrywhistle, who is a great favourite with them, and to whom such moments as these are the sweetest in his life. Charley tells over again the stirring incidents of the day, and they nod their heads, and laugh, and clap their hands, and cluster round him. Charley is their king.

'Come, children, sit down,' presently says Mr. Silver.

They sit round the table, Charley at the head, next to Mrs. Silver; then come Ruth and Rachel, with hands clasped beneath the tablecloth; then Mary and Richard. Mr. Silver produces a book; they hold their breaths. The blind girl knows that the book is on the table, and her fingers tighten upon Ruth's, and all her ears are in her eyes. It is a study to watch the varying shades of expression upon her face. As Mr. Silver opens the book you might hear a pin drop. Ruth nestles closer to Rachel, and Charley rises in his excitement. Mr. Merrywhistle sits in the armchair, and as he looks round upon the happy group, is as happy as the happiest among them. It is the custom every evening (unless pressing duties intervene) to read a chapter of a good work of fiction, and the reading-hour is looked forward to with eager delight by all the children. Last week they finished the Vicar of Wakefield, and this week they are introduced to the tender romance of Paul and Virginia. The selection of proper books is a grave task, and is always left to Mrs. Silver, who sometimes herself reads aloud.

'Where did we leave off last night, children?' asks Mr. Silver.

'Where Madame de la Tour receives a letter from her aunt,' answers Mary.

'Yes, from her spiteful old aunt,' adds Richard, 'and where Paul stamps his feet and wants to know who it is that has made Virginia's mother unhappy.'

A 'Hush-sh-sh!' runs round the table; and Mr. Silver commences the beautiful chapter where Virginia gives food to the poor slave woman, and induces her master to pardon her. With what eagerness do the children listen to how Paul and Virginia are lost in the woods! They gather cresses with the young lovers, and they help Paul set fire to the palm-tree, and they see the Three Peaks in the distance. Then they come to the famous part where Paul and Virginia stand by the banks of a river, the waters of which roll foaming over a bed of rocks. 'The noise of the water frightened Virginia, and she durst not wade through the stream; Paul therefore took her up in his arms, and went thus loaded over the slippery rocks, which formed the bed of the river, careless of the tumultuous noise of its waters.' [Thinks Richard, 'O, how I wish that I were Paul, carrying Virginia over the river!'] '"Do not be afraid," cried Paul to Virginia; "I feel very strong with you. If the inhabitant of the Black River had refused you the pardon of his slave, I would have fought with him."' ['And so would I,' thinks Richard, clenching his fists.] Night comes, and the lovers are almost despairing. Profound silence reigns in the awful solitudes. Will they escape? Can they escape? Paul climbs to the top of a tree, and cries, 'Come, come to the help of Virginia!' But only the echoes answer him, and the faint sound of 'Virginia, Virginia!' wanders through the forest. Despairing, they try to comfort each other, and seek for solace in prayer. Hark! they hear the barking of a dog. 'Surely,' says Virginia, 'it is Fidèle, our own dog. Yes, I know his voice. Are we, then, so near home? At the foot of our own mountain?' So they are rescued, and this night's reading ends happily. The delight of the children, the intense interest with which they hang upon every word, cannot be described. Their attention is so thoroughly engrossed, that the figures of the young lovers might be living and moving before them. When Mr. Silver shuts the book, a sigh comes from the youthful audience. A pause ensues, and then the children talk unreservedly about the story, and what the end will be--all but Ruth, who is too young yet to form opinions. It is of course this and of course that with them all, and not one of them guesses the truth, or has any idea of the tragic ending of the story.

'Charley,' says little Ruth, 'you are like Paul.'

They all clap their hands in acquiescence.

'But where's my Virginia?' asks Charley.

'I'll be Virginia,' cries Ruth somewhat precociously; 'and you can carry me about where you like.'

They all laugh at this, and Ruth is quite proud, believing that she has distinguished herself. It is strange to hear the blind girl say, 'I can see Paul with Virginia in his arms.' And no doubt she can, better than the others who are blessed with sight. The three grown-up persons listen and talk among themselves, and now and then join in the conversation. The clock strikes--nine. It is a cuckoo-clock, and the children listen to the measured 'Cuckoo! Cuck-oo!' until the soulless bird, having, with an egregious excess of vanity, asserted itself nine times as the great 'I am' of all the birds in town or country, retires into its nest, and sleeps for an hour. Then a chapter from the Bible and prayers, and in the prayers a few words to the memory of two--a brother and a sister--who have gone from among them. For last year they were seven; now they are five. Their faces grow sad as the memory of their dear brother and sister comes upon them in their prayers, and 'Poor Archie!' 'Poor Lizzie!' hang upon their lips. The night's pleasures and duties being ended, the three youngest children go to bed, the last kind nod and smile being given to Ruth, sister to poor Blade-o'-Grass, who lingers a moment behind the others, and with her arm round Rachel's neck, cries 'Cuck-oo! Cuck-oo!' as her final good-night. But the proud bird in the clock takes no notice, and preserves a disdainful silence, although Ruth, as her custom is, waits a moment or two, and listens for the reply that does not come. Charley and Mary stop up an hour later than the others, reading; but before that hour expires, Mr. Merrywhistle bids his friends good-night, and retires.

MR. MERRYWHISTLE MEETS THE QUEER LITTLE OLD MAN.

But not to his bed. He was restless, and, the night being a fine one, he strolled out of Buttercup-square into the quiet streets. It was a favourite custom of his to walk along the streets of a night with no companions but his thoughts. Almost invariably he chose the quiet streets, for there are streets in London--north and south and east and west--which never sleep; streets which are healthy with traffic in the day, and diseased with traffic in the night.

Mr. Merrywhistle walked along and mused, in no unhappy frame of mind. A visit to the Silvers always soothed and comforted him; and on this occasion the sweet face of Mrs. Silver, and the happy faces and voices of the children, rested upon him like a peaceful cloud. So engrossed was he, that he did not heed the pattering of a small urchin at his side, and it was many moments before he awoke from his walking dream, and became conscious of the importunate intruder.

'If you please, sir!' said the small urchin, for the twentieth time, in a voice of weak pleading.

Mr. Merrywhistle looked down, and saw a face that he fancied he had seen before. But the memory of the happy group in Buttercup-square still lingered upon him. What he really saw as he looked down was a little boy without a cap, large-eyed, white-faced, and bare-footed. No other than Tom Beadle in fact, making hay, or trying to make it, not while the sun, but while the moon shone.

'If you please, sir!' repeated the boy, 'will you give me a copper to buy a bit o' bread?'

Then the dawn of faint suspicion loomed upon Mr. Merrywhistle. He placed his hand lightly upon Tom Beadle's shoulder, and said in a troubled voice, 'My boy, haven't I seen you before to-day?'

'No, sir,' boldly answered Tom Beadle, having no suspicion of the truth; for when the shilling was slipped into his hand, his eyes were towards the ground, and he did not see Mr. Merrywhistle's face.

'Were you not on the Royal Exchange with a little girl, and didn't I give you a--a shilling?'

For a moment Tom Beadle winced, and he had it in his mind to twist his shoulder from Mr. Merrywhistle's grasp and run away. For a moment only: natural cunning and his inclination kept him where he was. To tell the honest truth, a lie was a sweet morsel to Tom Beadle, and he absolutely gloried in 'taking people in.' So, on this occasion, he sent one sharp glance at Mr. Merrywhistle--which, rapid as it was, had all the effect of a sun-picture upon him--and whined piteously, 'Me 'ave a shillin' guv to me! Never 'ad sich a bit o' luck in all my born days. It was some other boy, sir, some cove who didn't want it. They allus gits the luck of it. And as for a little gal and the Royal Igschange, I wish I may die if I've been near the place for a week!'

'And you are hungry?' questioned Mr. Merrywhistle, fighting with his doubts.

"Aven't 'ad a ounce o' bread in my mouth this blessed day;' and two large tears gathered in Tom Beadle's eyes. He took care that Mr. Merrywhistle should see them.

Mr. Merrywhistle sighed, and with a feeling of positive pain gave twopence to Tom Beadle, who slipped his shoulder from Mr. Merrywhistle's hand with the facility of an eel, and scudded away in an exultant frame of mind.

Mr. Merrywhistle walked a few steps, hesitated, and then turned in the direction that Tom Beadle had taken.

'Now, I wonder,' he thought, 'whether the collector was right this morning, and whether I have been assisting in making criminals today.'

Truly this proved to be a night of coincidences to Mr. Merrywhistle; for he had not walked a mile before he came upon the queer little old man, whom he had met on the Royal Exchange. The old fellow was leaning against a lamp-post, smoking a pipe, and seemed to be as much at home in the wide street as he would have been in his own parlour. He looked surly and ill-grained, and his eyebrows were very precipitous. His mild eye was towards Mr. Merrywhistle, as that gentleman approached him, and when Mr. Merrywhistle slowly passed him, his fierce eye came in view and lighted upon the stroller. Before he had left the old man three yards behind him, Mr. Merrywhistle fancied he heard a chuckle. He would have dearly liked to turn back and accost the old man, but a feeling of awkwardness was upon him, and he could not muster sufficient courage. Chance, however, brought about an interview. Not far from him was a building that might have been a palace, it was so grand and light. It was a triumph of architecture, with its beautiful pillars, and its elaborate stonework. Great windows, higher than a man's height, gilt framed, and blazing with a light that threw everything around them in the shade, tempted the passer-by to stop and admire. There were three pictures in the windows, and these pictures were so cunningly surrounded by jets of light, that they could not fail to attract the eye. Awful satires were these pictures. Two of them represented the figure of a man under different aspects. On the left, this man was represented with a miserably-attenuated face, every line in which expressed woe and destitution; his clothes were so ragged that his flesh peeped through; his cheeks were thin, his lips were drawn in, his eyes were sunken; his lean hands seemed to tremble beneath a weight of misery: at the foot of this picture was an inscription, to the effect that it was the portrait of a man who did not drink So-and-so's gin and So-and-so's stout, both of which life's elixirs were to be obtained within. On the right, this same man was represented with full-fleshed face, with jovial eyes, with handsome mouth and teeth, with plump cheeks, with fat hands--his clothes and everything about him betokening worldly prosperity and happiness: at the foot of this picture was an inscription, to the effect that it was the portrait of the same man who (having, it is to be presumed, seen the error of his ways) did drink So-and-so's gin and So-and-so's stout. A glance inside this palace, crowded with Misery, would have been sufficient to show what a bitter satire these pictures were. But the centre picture, in addition to being a bitter satire, was awfully suggestive. It was this:

Whether to the artist or to the manufacturer was due the credit of ingeniously parading 'Old Tom' in a coffin, cannot (through the ignorance of the writer) here be recorded. But there it shone--an ominous advertisement. As Mr. Merrywhistle halted for a moment before these pictures, there issued from the Laboratory of Crime and Disease a man and a woman: he, blotched and bloated; she, worn-eyed and weary--both of them in rags. The woman, clinging to his arm, was begging him to come home--for his sake; for hers; for the children's; for God's! With his disengaged hand he struck at her, and she fell to the ground, bleeding. She rose, however, and wiped her face with her apron, and implored him again and again to come home--and again he struck at her: this time with cruel effect, for she lay in the dust, helpless for a while. A crowd gathered quickly, and a hubbub ensued. In the midst of the Babel of voices, Mr. Merrywhistle, looking down saw the strange old man standing by his side. The same surly, sneering expression was on the old man's countenance, and Mr. Merrywhistle felt half inclined to quarrel with him for it. But before he had time to speak, the old man took the pipe out of his mouth, and pointing the stem in the direction of the chief actors in the scene, said, 'I knew them two when they was youngsters.'

'Indeed,' replied Mr. Merrywhistle, interested immediately, and delighted at the opportunity of opening up the conversation.

'She was a han'some gal; you'd scarce believe it to look at her now. She 'ad eyes like sloes; though whether sloes is bird, beast, or fish, I couldn't tell ye, but I've heard the sayin' a 'undred times. Anyways, she 'ad bright black eyes, and was a good gal too; but she fell in love'--(in a tone of intense scorn)--with that feller, and married him, the fool!'

'What has brought them to this?'

'Gin!' said the old man, expelling the word as if it were a bullet, and bringing his fierce eye to bear with all its force upon Mr. Merrywhistle.

Short as was the time occupied by this dialogue, it was long enough to put an end to the scene before them. The woman was raised to her feet by other women, many of whom urged her to 'Give him in charge, the brute!' but she shook her head, and staggered away in pain. Very quickly after her disappearance the crowd dissolved, by far the greater part of it finding its way through the swing-doors of the gin-palace, to talk of the event over So-and-so's gin and So-and-so's stout. Not that there was anything new or novel in the occurrence. It was but a scene in a drama of real life that had been played many hundred times in that locality. Presently the street was quite clear, and Mr. Merrywhistle and the old man were standing side by side, alone. A handy lamp-post served as a resting-place for the old man, who continued to smoke his pipe, and to chuckle between whiles, as if he knew that Mr. Merrywhistle wanted to get up a conversation, and did not know how to commence. As he saw that the old man was determined not to assist him, and as every moment added to the awkwardness of the situation, Mr. Merrywhistle made a desperate plunge.

'When I was on the Royal Exchange to-day----' he commenced.

The old man took his pipe out of his mouth, and expelled a cloud and a chuckle at the same moment.

'I thought you was a-comin' to that,' he said. 'You owe me a bob.'

'What for?'

'I made a bet with you--to myself--that the first thing you'd speak about was the Royal Exchange. I bet you a bob--to myself--and I won it.'

Without hesitation Mr. Merrywhistle took a shilling from his pocket, and offered it to the old man, who eyed it with his fierce eye for a moment, doubtingly and with curiosity, and then calmly took possession of it, and put it in his waistcoat-pocket.

'When you was, on the Royal Exchange to-day,' he said, repeating Mr. Merrywhistle's words, 'you sor a boy and a girl a-beggin'.'

'No,' exclaimed Mr. Merrywhistle warmly; 'they were not begging.'

'You may call it what you like,' said the old man; 'but I call it beggin'; and so would that identical boy, if I was to ask him. He wouldn't tell you so, though. The boy he looked as if he was goin' to die, and you give him a copper or a bit of silver; and you wasn't pleased because I laughed at you for it. Now, then, fire away.'

'Was that boy starving? Was he as ill as he looked? Was I----'

'Took in?' added the old man, as Mr. Merrywhistle hesitated to express the doubt 'Why? D'ye want your money back? Lord! he's a smart little chap, is Tom Beadle!'

'You know him, then?'

'Know him!' replied the old man, with a contemptuous snort; 'I'd like to be told who it is about 'ere I don't know. And I'd like to know who you are. I'm almost as fond of askin' questions as I am of answering 'em. What's sauce for the goose is sauce for the gander. If you expect Jimmy Wirtue to answer your questions, you must make up your mind to answer his'n.'

'You're Mr. Virtue, then?'

'You're at it agin. No, I'm not Mr. Virtue' (he had to struggle with the 'V' before it would pass his lips), 'but Jimmy Wirtue--and that's not Jimmy Wice. What's your'n?'

'Merrywhistle,' replied that gentleman shortly.

Jimmy Virtue was pleased at the quick answer.

'Merrywhistle!' he exclaimed. 'That's a rum name--rummer than mine. What more would you like to know? What am I? I keep a leavin'-shop. Where do I live? In Stoney-alley. Now, what are you; and where do you live? Are you a Methody parson, or a penny-a-liner, or a detective, or a cove that goes about studyin' human nater, or a feelanthrofist. We've lots o' them knockin' about 'ere.'

Mr. Merrywhistle was constrained to reply, but found himself unexpectedly in a quandary.

'I'm a--a--O, I'm Nothing Particular,' blurting it out almost in desperation.

'You look like it,' chuckled Jimmy Virtue, so tickled by his smart retort as to be satisfied with Mr. Merrywhistle's vague definition of his calling. 'We've lots of your sort, too, knockin' about here--more than the feelanthrofists, I shouldn't wonder. But I don't think there's any 'arm in you. Jimmy Wirtue's not a bad judge of a face; and he can tell you every one of your organs. 'Ere's Benevolence--you've got that large; 'ere's Ideality--not much o' that; 'ere's Language--shut your eyes; 'ere's Causality--no, it ain't; you 'aven't got it. I can't see your back bumps, nor the bumps atop o' your 'ead; but I could ferret out every one of 'em, if I 'ad my fingers there.'

At this moment an individual approached them who would have attracted the attention of the most unobservant. Mr. Merrywhistle did not see his face; but the gait of the man was so singular, that his eyes wandered immediately in the direction of the man. At every three steps the singular figure paused, and puffed, as if he were a steam-engine, and was blowing off steam. One--two--three; puff. One--two--three; puff. One--two--three; puff.

'What on earth is the matter with the man?' exclaimed Mr. Merrywhistle to Jimmy Virtue.

'Nothing that I knows of,' replied Jimmy Virtue; 'he's been goin' on that way for the last twenty year. If you're lookin' out for characters, you'll get plenty of 'em 'ere. Perhaps you're a artist for one of the rubbishy picter-papers--one of the fellers who sees a murder done in a Whitechapel court one day, and takes a picter of it on the spot from nater; and who sees a shipwreck in the Atlantic the next day, and takes a picter of that on the spot from nater. That there man's worth his ten 'undred golden sovereigns a-year, if he's worth a penny; and he lives on tuppence a-day. The girls and boys about here calls him Three-Steps-and-a-Puff. If you was to go and offer him a ha'penny, he'd take it.'

By the time that Three-Steps-and-a-Puff was out of sight, the tobacco in Jimmy Virtue's pipe had turned to dust and smoke, and he prepared to depart also. But seeing that Mr. Merrywhistle was inclined for further conversation, he said:

'Perhaps you'd like to come down and see my place?'

Mr. Merrywhistle said that he would very much like to come down and see Jimmy Virtue's place.

'Come along, then,' said Jimmy Virtue, but paused, and said, 'Stop a bit; perhaps you wouldn't mind buyin' a penn'orth o' baked taters first.'

A baked-potato can, with a man attached to it, being near them, Mr. Merrywhistle invested a penny, thinking that Jimmy Virtue intended the potatoes for supper.

'Did you ever consider,' said the eccentric old man, as they turned down the narrowest of lanes, 'that a big city was like a theaytre?'

'No, it never struck me.'

'It is, though I there's stalls, and dress-circle, and pit, and gallery, in a big city like London. The west, that's the stalls and private boxes; the north, that's the dress-circle; the south, that's the pit; the east, that's the gallery. This is the penny-gallery of the theaytre; 'taint a nice place to lay in.'

He stopped before the forms of two children--a boy and a girl--who, huddled in each other's arms, were fast asleep in a gateway. He stirred them gently with his foot; and the boy started to his feet instantaneously, wide awake, and on the alert for his natural enemies, the police. Mr. Merrywhistle was standing in the abutment of the gateway, and the boy couldn't see his face; but the well-known form of Jimmy Virtue was instantly recognised; and as the boy sank to the ground, he muttered:

'What's the good of waking us up just as we was a-gettin' warm? You wouldn't like it yourself, Mr. Wirtue, you wouldn't.'

Then he crept closer to his companion, and said sleepily:

'Come along, Bladergrass; let's turn in agin.'

The girl, who had been regarding the two dark shadows with a half-frightened, half-imploring look, as if she dreaded that they were about to turn her out of her miserable shelter, nestled in the lad's arms, and the next minute they were asleep again. All blessings were not denied to them.

'I know that lad,' said Mr. Merrywhistle.

'You ought to; it's Tom Beadle.'

'And he was at the Royal Exchange to-day with that poor little girl?'

'Yes, that was him. You thought he was dyin'. What do you think now?

Jimmy Virtue seemed to take positive pleasure in putting the affair in the worst light.

Mr. Merrywhistle did not answer the question, but said, in a sad tone, 'He begged of me again to-night.'

'Did he, though!' exclaimed Jimmy Virtue admiringly.

'And when I asked him if any one had given him a--a shilling on the Royal Exchange to-day, he took an oath that he hadn't been near the Royal Exchange for a month, and that he had never had a shilling given to him in all his life.'

'And did you believe him, and give him anythin'?'

'Yes' (hesitatingly), 'I gave him a trifle.'

Jimmy Virtue stopped by a post, and held his sides. When he had had his laugh out, he said:

'Tom's a smart little thief. But you're not the first gent he's taken in twice in one day. Come, now, he's taken you in twice with your eyes shut; let him take you in once more with your eyes open.'

'I don't understand.'

'Them baked taters--'

'Well?'

'It wouldn't be a bad thing--like returnin' good for evil, as the preachers say--if you was to go and put them taters in the little girl's lap.'

'No--no--no!' exclaimed Mr. Merrywhistle, a little violently, and pausing between each negative, 'it'll be paying a premium for dishonesty and lies.'

The good fellow's heart was filled with pain as he uttered these words, which, hotly spoken, served as fuel to flame; for Jimmy Virtue turned upon him almost savagely, and snarled:

'You're a nice article, you are, a-givin' and repentin'! I've been took in by you, I 'ave. If I 'ad my fingers on the back o' your 'ead, I'd find something that would do away with your bumps o' benevolence. Dishonesty and lies! What'd you want, you and the likes? The boy's got to live, ain't he? The boy's got to eat, ain't he? If he can't work and don't beg, what's he to do? Steal? Yah! D'you think he's got money in the bank? D'you think, if he 'ad his pockets full, he'd sleep in the open air, in a gateway?'

'Stop, stop, my good friend!' implored Mr. Merrywhistle, overcome by remorse at his hard-heartedness. He ran quickly to where the children were lying, and deposited the baked potatoes, and a few coppers as well, in the girl's lap and hands. When he came back to where Jimmy Virtue was standing, he found that worthy only half mollified.

'A-givin' and repentin',' muttered the old man, as he walked towards Stoney-alley, 'that's a nice kind o' charity!' Impelled by a sudden thought, he turned back to the gateway, and kneeling by the side of Blade-o'-Grass, opened her hot hand in which the pence were.

'He's not a bad chap, after all,' he murmured, as he retraced his steps, 'but it's enough to rile a feller and put a feller's back up, when a man gives and repents.'

JIMMY VIRTUE INTRODUCES MR. MERRYWHISTLE TO HIS PLACE OF BUSINESS.

The moment Mr. Merrywhistle entered the habitation of Jimmy Virtue he felt as if he were mildewed, and an impression stole upon him that he had been lying on a musty shelf for a dozen years at least, and had not been washed during the whole of the time. The place was dark when they entered, and as Mr. Merrywhistle advanced cautiously, he came in contact with soft bundles, from which a mouldy smell proceeded, and which so encompassed him on all sides, that he was frightened at every step he moved, lest he should bring confusion on himself. When Jimmy Virtue lighted two melancholy wicks-- tallow twelves--Mr. Merrywhistle looked about him in wonder. It was the queerest and the dirtiest of shops, and was filled with bundles of rags. Pocket-handkerchiefs, trousers, coats, waistcoats, and underclothing of every description met his eye whichever way he turned; faded dresses and dirty petticoats (many with mud still on them, as if they had been taken off in the streets in bad weather) so choked the shelves, that some of them were in danger of bursting out; old boots hung from the ceiling; old crinolines loomed upon him from the unlikeliest of places, and, as he looked timorously up at them, yawned to ingulf him. One, hanging behind the parlour-door, in the gloomiest corner, was so disposed, that Mr. Merrywhistle's disturbed fancy added the lines of a woman's form hanging in it; and the fancy grew so strong upon him, that although he turned his back to the spot immediately, he could not dismiss the figure of the hanging woman from his imagination. There was an apartment behind the shop which Jimmy Virtue called his parlour; but that was almost as full of rubbish as the shop. Neither in shop or parlour was there fairly room to turn round in; if you wanted to perform that movement, you had to tack for it.

'And this is your dwelling,' Observed Mr. Merrywhistle, feeling it incumbent upon him to speak, as Jimmy Virtue led the way into the parlour, and motioned him to a seat.

'I don't call it by that name myself,' replied Jimmy Virtue, in a not over-polite tone. 'It's where I live and gets my livin', and I don't give you more than a quarter of an hour.'

By which Mr. Merrywhistle understood, that beyond a quarter of an hour it would not be politeness for him to stay.

'Ever been in a leavin'-shop before?' asked the old man.

'No,' replied Mr. Merrywhistle; 'not that I am aware of. May I ask you what a leaving-shop is?'

'This is,' said Jimmy. 'All them things you see in the shop and in the parlour--all them crinolines and peddicuts, and boots and dresses-- belongs to poor people round about 'ere. I lend 'em a trifle on 'em, and takes care of 'em; and charges 'em a trifle when they take 'em out.'

'They don't seem worth much,' observed Mr. Merrywhistle reflectively.

'Perhaps not--to you. But they're worth a deal to them they belongs to. There's a many o' them crinolines and peddicuts that comes in and out like a Jack-in-a-box. Their movements are as regular as clockwork. Monday afternoon in, Sunday mornin' out.'

Here, to Mr. Merrywhistle's consternation, Jimmy Virtue took out his mild eye--it being a glass one--and with the laconic remark, 'A damp night makes it clammy,' wiped it calmly, and put it in again. The effect of this upon Mr. Merrywhistle was appalling. To see that mild eye--knowing that it was a glass one, and that a damp night made it clammy--side by side with that fierce eye which, as he had described, seemed inclined to fly out of its owner's head at you, was almost too much for human endurance. And as Mr. Merrywhistle looked at them--he could not help doing so, there was such a fascination in them--both eyes seemed to glare at him, and the glare of the glass was more dreadful and overpowering than the glare of the flesh. Jimmy Virtue, whose one organ of sight was as potent as if he were Argus-eyed, remarked Mr. Merrywhistle's perturbation, and quietly enjoyed it; he did not refer to the subject, however, but considerately treated Mr. Merrywhistle to as much of his glass eye as he could conveniently bestow upon him.

'Speakin' of crinolines and peddicuts,' observed Jimmy, recurring to his stock, 'they're not the only women's things that's left. We're in the fashion down 'ere, I can tell you. In that box that you're a-settin' on, there's a matter of seven chinons, that I takes care of regularly a week-days--real 'air three of 'em are; them as belongs to 'em I do believe would sooner go without their stockin's a Sundays than without their chinons. And now, jumpin' from one thing to another, I should like to know whether you've got over your repentin' fit, and whether you think Tom Beadle ought to be put in quod for takin' your shillin' to-day.'

'No; I've no doubt he did it out of necessity. But I wish he hadn't told me----'

'Lies. Don't stop at the word. Out of necessity! Ay, I should think he did, the clever little thief. And necessity's the mother of invention--consequently, necessity's the mother o' lies. You want a friend o' mine to talk to you. He'd argue with you; but I fly into a passion, and ain't got the patience that he's got. He'd talk to you about Tom Beadle and little Blade-o'-Grass, and put things in a way that ud stun you to 'ear.'

'Little what?'

'Blade-o'-Grass--the little girl that's sleepin' with Tom Beadle in the gateway.'

'What a singular name!--has she a mother and father?'

'No mother; I can't say about father. I remember him before the young uns was born. He lived in this alley, and used to come into the shop and leave his wife's things, and talk about the rights of man. The rights of man! I tell you what he thought of them: a little while before his wife was brought to bed, he cut away and left her. She was brought to bed with twins--girls--and after that, she died.'

'Then Blade-o'-Grass has a sister?'

'Who said she 'as? I didn't. No, she ain't got a sister. I don't know what came o' the other; but that don't matter to Blade-o'-Grass. Here she is, poor little devil, and that's enough for her, and more than enough, I'll take my davy on. Time's up.'

This was an intimation that it was time for Mr. Merrywhistle to take his departure. Wishing to stand well in the eyes of Jimmy Virtue--notwithstanding the dreadful effect the glass eye had upon him--he rose, and said that he hoped they would meet again; to which Jimmy Virtue said, that he had no objection.

'What do you say, now,' suggested Mr. Merrywhistle, 'to you and your friend that you would like to talk to me coming to take a cup of tea or a bit of dinner with me?'

'Which?' asked Jimmy Virtue. 'Tea I don't care for.'

'Dinner, then.'

'A good dinner?'

'Yes.'

'Wine?'

'Yes.'

Something very like a twinkle shone in the old man's fierce eye. He rubbed his hand over his chin, and said,

'It's worth considerin' on.--When?'

'Next Saturday; any time in the afternoon you like to name.'

'That ud suit my friend,' said Jimmy Virtue, evidently impressed by the prospect of a good dinner; 'he leaves off work a Saturdays at two o'clock----'

'Then we'll consider it settled,' said Mr. Merrywhistle eagerly.

'----But I don't know that it ud suit me,' continued Jimmy, the twinkle vanishing, and a calculating look taking its place. 'There's the shop. I'd 'ave to shut it up--and then what would the customers do? To be sure, I could put up a notice sayin' that it ud be open at nine o'clock. I keep open till twelve Saturday night.'

'Very well; manage it that way.'

'I think you told me that you was Nothink Particular when I asked you what you was, and bein' Nothink Particular, time's no account to you. Now it is some account to me--it's money.' Here he turned his blind eye to Mr. Merrywhistle. 'If you want me to shut up my shop for six hours, say, you must make it up to me. If you want Jimmy Wirtue's company, you must pay for Jimmy Wirtue's time.'

'That's fair enough,' said Mr. Merrywhistle readily, scarcely hearing the suppressed chuckle to which Jimmy Virtue gave vent at the answer. 'What do you value your time at?

'Sixpence an hour--three shillings for the six hours. Then there's the disappointment to the customers, and the injury to the business; but I'll throw them in.'

Without a word, Mr. Merrywhistle took three shillings from his pocket and placed them on the table. Still keeping his blind side to Mr. Merrywhistle, Jimmy Virtue tried the coins with his teeth, and said, 'Done!'

Whether he meant that he had 'done' Mr. Merrywhistle, or that the word referred to the binding of the invitation to dinner, he did not stop to explain, but asked,

'Where?'

'At the Three Jolly Butcher Boys, Cannon-street,' replied Mr. Merrywhistle, not being confident that the resources of his establishment in Buttercup-square would be sufficient to satisfy his new and eccentric acquaintance.

'That's settled, then,' said Jimmy, 'and I'll bring my friend at four o'clock. And now, if you don't mind takin' a bit of advice, take this--never you go talkin' to strangers agin at such a time o' night as this, and never you accept another invitation to visit a man you don't know nothin' of.'

'But I knew I could trust you,' said Mr. Merrywhistle, smiling.

'Did you!' exclaimed Jimmy. 'Then I wouldn't give the snuff of a candle for your judgment. I'll see you out of this, if you please.'

So saying, he led his visitor out of the shop. Mr. Merrywhistle could not, for the life of him, help casting a hurried glance over his shoulder in the direction of the special crinoline which had so distressed him; and again the fancy came upon him, that he saw a woman hanging behind the door. When he was in the open, however, this fancy vanished, and he breathed more freely. They stopped to look at the sleeping forms of Tom Beadle and Blade-o'-Grass in the gateway. The children were fast locked in each other's arms, and were sleeping soundly.

In the wider thoroughfare, Jimmy Virtue bade Mr. Merrywhistle 'good-night,' and as he walked back to his shop in Stoney-alley, amused himself by polishing his glass eye with a dirty pocket-handkerchief, and chuckling over the remembrances of the night.

In the mean time, Mr. Merrywhistle made his way to Buttercup-square, not ill pleased with his adventure. But in the night he was tormented by singular dreams, the most striking one of which contained the horrible incident of Jimmy Virtue glaring at him with his glass eye, and swallowing at one gulp a huge baked potato, with Tom Beadle and Blade-o'-Grass sticking in the middle of it.

THE STRANGE IDEA OF HALLELUJAH ENTERTAINED BY BLADE-O'-GRASS.

Punctually at four o'clock oh Saturday, Jimmy Virtue, accompanied by his friend, presented himself to Mr. Merrywhistle at the Three Jolly Butcher Boys. It might reasonably have been expected, that Jimmy would have made some change for the better in his appearance, in honour of the occasion; but Mr. Merrywhistle fancied that, out of defiance, Jimmy had allowed the accumulated dust of days to lie thick upon his clothes, and that he had purposely neglected to brush them. Indeed, he almost asserted as much by his manner: You saw what I was, and you forced yourself upon me; you invited me and my friend to dinner, and you must take the consequences. His only eye, as it blazed at Mr. Merrywhistle from under its precipice of bushy hair, seemed to be asking of that gentleman how he liked its owner's appearance: and it softened somewhat in the kindly glances from Mr. Merrywhistle, whose countenance was beaming with amiability and good-nature.

'This is my friend that I spoke of,' said Jimmy Virtue; 'his name is Truefit, Robert Truefit. Truefit by name, and Truefit by nature. This is Mr. Merrywhistle, who sometimes gives and repents.'

Robert Truefit came forward, with a manly bow, and, when Mr. Merrywhistle offered his hand, shook it cordially.

'My friend, Mr. Virtue, here--' he said, and was about to proceed, when the old man struck in with,

'Now, I won't have it. Bob; I won't have it. None of your misters because we're before company. It's Jimmy Wirtue when we are alone, and it's Jimmy Wirtue now; and if you're a-goin' to say anythin' in apology for me, don't. I don't want apologies made for me, and I won't 'ave 'em.'

Robert Truefit laughed, and said, 'We must let old Jimmy have his way, sir, so I won't say what I was going to say.' Robert Truefit was about thirty years of age, and was a stonemason by trade. He had a shrewd intelligent face and clear brown eyes, which, young as he was, already showed the signs of much thought. He was as manly a fellow as you would wish to look upon, and in his speech and manner there was a straightforwardness which at once won for him the good opinion of those with whom he came in contact. So conspicuous was this straightforwardness of speech and manner, that he was often called Straightforward Bob by his comrades and those who knew him intimately. Directly you set eyes upon him, you received the impression, not only that he was a man to be depended upon, but that he was one who was apt to form his own opinions, and would stand by them through thick and thin, unless absolutely convinced, through his reason, that they were wrong. He had a wife who adored him, and children who looked up to him in love and respect, as to a king. He was a true type of English manhood and English shrewd common sense.

By the time the few words were exchanged, dinner was on the table, and Mr. Merrywhistle motioned his guests to be seated. But Jimmy Virtue, turning his blind eye to his host, said, with an odd smile, 'I've got two more friends outside. May I bring them in?'

Without waiting for Mr. Merrywhistle's consent, he went to the door and brought forward Tom Beadle and Blade-o'-Grass. Presenting them to Mr. Merrywhistle, he went through a kind of mock introduction. Mr. Thomas Beadle, Miss Blade-o'-Grass, Mr. Merrywhistle.

Tom Beadle made an awkward bow, and Blade-o'-Grass made a still more awkward curtsey. Blade-o'-Grass was the only one of the four guests who had thought fit to do honour to the occasion in the matter of dress. Jimmy Virtue, as you have seen, had made himself shabbier than usual; Robert Truefit was in his working clothes; and it would have been simply impossible for Tom Beadle to have made any change in his garments, unless he had stolen them, or had had them given to him. But Blade-o'-Grass, who, like Tom Beadle, possessed no other clothes than those she stood upright in--and those were as ragged as clothes could be--had by some strange means acquired a bonnet, and it was on her head now. Such a bonnet! If it had been gifted with a tongue, it could doubtless have told a strange story of its career. For although now it was only fit for a dunghill, it had been a fine bonnet once, and, torn and soiled as it was, the semblance of a once fashionable shape was still dimly recognisable. But Blade-o'-Grass was proud of it, wrecked and fallen as it was from its high estate.

Now it may as well be confessed at once, that Tom Beadle was not at his ease. When he had made his awkward bow, he raised his eyes to the face of Mr. Merrywhistle, and recognised him. He did not know where he was going to when Jimmy Virtue had asked him if he would like to have a good dinner; and when he recognised Mr. Merrywhistle, he sent a reproachful look at Jimmy Virtue, and involuntarily squared his arms and elbows to ward off the knock on the head he expected to receive. But as Jimmy Virtue only chuckled (knowing the fear that possessed Tom Beadle), and as Mr. Merrywhistle was gentleness itself, the lad, after a time, became reassured--though he still kept his elbows ready.

'You sit down in the corner,' said Jimmy Virtue to the children, 'and when we've finished dinner, you may eat what's left.'

'Nay,' said Mr. Merrywhistle, chiming in with the humour of his guest; 'there is more than enough for all. Let them eat with us.' And he placed the children at the table, where they sat watching the filling of their plates with gloating wonderment.

'Stop a minute, young uns,' said Jimmy Virtue, arresting their uplifted forks, which they were clumsily handling, 'Grace before meat. Repeat after me: For this bit o' luck----'

'For this bit o'luck,' they repeated.

'Let us say----' he.

'Let us say----' they.

'Hallelujah!'

'Alleloojah.'

'Now, you can fire away.'

And fire away they did, eating as hungry children only can eat--never lifting their heads once from their plates until they had cleaned them out; then they looked up for more.

Jimmy Virtue was quite as busily employed as the children, and ate and drank with an air of intense enjoyment. Robert Truefit had more leisure. He ate very little, having had his dinner at one o'clock. Scarcely any conversation took place until dinner was over. Tom Beadle and Blade-o'-Grass had eaten their fill, but they still held their knives and forks in their hands, and looked eagerly at the remains of the meal. Jimmy Virtue's face had a purplish tinge on it, and his fierce eye had a mellow light in it, as he saw the children looking eagerly at the food.

'What was it you found in your' lap the other mornin'?' he asked of Blade-o'-Grass.

'Nothin',' was the reply.

'Not baked taters?

'No; we didn't 'ave 'em in the mornin'. Tom and me woke up in the middle o' the night, and eat 'em.'

'Wasn't you astonished to find baked taters in your lap when you woke up?'

'No; we was pleased.'

'Do you know who put 'em there?'

'The baked-tater man?' asked Blade-o'-Grass, after a little consideration.

'No; it wasn't him. Guess agin.'

Blade-o'-Grass considered, and shook her head; but suddenly a gleam lighted up her face. She pulled Tom Beadle to her, and whispered in his ear.

'She ses, if yer please,' said Tom, 'that p'r'aps it was Alleloojah.'

At this suggestion, Jimmy Virtue was seized with one of his fits of noiseless laughter; but both Mr. Merrywhistle and Robert Truefit looked grave. Blade-o'-Grass and Tom Beadle saw nothing either grave or ludicrous in the suggestion, for their attention was fully occupied in the contemplation of the food that was on the table. Mr. Merrywhistle, who was observing their rapt contemplation of the remains of the feast, observed also Jimmy Virtue's fiery eye regarding him.

'It's your'n? questioned the old man of his host.

'Yes, I suppose so.'

'You pay for it, whether it's eat or not?'

'Yes.'

'Give it to the young uns.'

'How win they take it away?'

'In a newspaper.'

Sharp Tom Beadle followed every word of the dialogue, and his lynx eyes were the first that saw a newspaper on a sofa in the room. He jumped from his seat, and brought forward the paper, his eyes glistening with hope. Mr. Merrywhistle and Jimmy Virtue wrapped up what remained of the joint of meat in the newspaper.

'Food for mind and body,' said Robert Truefit, as the parcel was given to Tom.

Tom ducked his head, without in the least knowing what Robert Truefit meant--and not caring either. His great anxiety was, to get away now that he had as much as was likely to be given to him. Blade-o'-Grass shared his anxiety. The gift of the food was such a splendid one--there really was a large quantity of meat left on the joint--that she feared it was only given to them 'out of a lark,' as she would have expressed it, and that it would be taken from them presently. A premonition was upon her, that she would be hungry to-morrow.

The children stood in painful suspense before the grown-up persons. Their anxiety to be dismissed was so great, that they threw restless glances around them, and shuffled uneasily with their feet. But Mr. Merrywhistle had something to say first. He had great difficulty in commencing, however. He coughed, and hesitated, and almost blushed, and looked at Jimmy Virtue in a shame-faced kind of way.

'The other day,' at length he commenced, addressing himself to Tom Beadle, 'when I saw you and Blade-o'-Grass on the Royal Exchange----'

Tom, in the most unblushing manner, was about to asseverate, upon his soul and body, that he was not near the Royal Exchange, when Jimmy Virtue's warning finger, and Jimmy Virtue's ominous eye, stopped the lie on his lips.

'----On the Royal Exchange,' continued Mr. Merrywhistle, 'and gave you--a--a shilling, were you really ill, as you seemed to me to be?'

A look of triumphant delight flashed into Tom Beadle's eyes. 'Did I. do it well, sir? he cried, nudging Blade-o'-Grass. 'Did I look as if I was a-dyin' by inches?'

Mr. Merrywhistle winced, as if he had received a blow.

'O, Tom, Tom!' he exclaimed gently, 'are you not ashamed of yourself?'

'No,' answered Tom, without hesitation, his manner instantly changing.

Blade-o'-Grass perceiving, with her quick instinct, that something was wrong, and that Tom was likely to get into disgrace because he had made the gentleman believe that he was dying by inches, stepped forward chivalrously to the rescue.

'If you please, sir,' she said, 'you mus'n't blame Tom. It was all along o' me he did it.'

Thereupon the following colloquy took place:

Robert Truefit. Bravo, Blade-o'-Grass!

Mr. Merrywhistle [only too ready to receive justification]. Come here, child. How was it all along of you?

Tom Beadle [taking moral shelter behind Blade-o'-Grass]. Tell the gent the truth, Bladergrass; he won't 'urt you. Tell him about the tiger.

Mr. Merrywhistle [in amazement]. The tiger!

Blade-o'-Grass [gravely]. Yes, sir; I got a tiger in my inside.

Mr. Merrywhistle. Who on earth put such a monstrous idea into the child's head?

Blade-o'-Grass. Mr. Wirtue knows all about it, and so does all the others in Stoney-alley.

Jimmy Virtue [nodding gravely in confirmation]. Yes, she's got a tiger. Tell the gentleman what it does to you, Blade-o'-Grass.

Blade-o'-Grass. Eats up everythink as goes down my throat, sir; swallers every blessed bit I puts in my mouth; and when I ain't got nothink to give it, tears at me like one o'clock. Tom's giv me grub for it orfen and orfen, sir; I don't know what I should a' done lots o' times if it 'adn't been for 'im. [Mr. Merrywhistle sheds a kindly glance on Tom Beadle, who receives it with an air of injured innocence.] Well, sir, last Monday the tiger was a'-goin' on orfle, and I was so sick that I begins to cry. Then Tom comes up, and arks me what I'm cryin' for; and I tells 'im that the tiger's a-worryin' the inside out o' me. Tom feels in 'is pockets, but he ain't got a copper to giv me, so he ses, 'Come along o' me,' ses Tom; and he ketches 'old of my 'and, and takes me to the Royal Igschange. Then he ses, ses Tom, 'If anybody arks you, Bladergrass, just you say that I'm your brother, a-dyin' of consumption. I'm a-dyin' by inches, I am.' And I cries out, sir, for Tom looked jist as if he was a-dyin' by inches. [A smile of triumph wreathes Tom Beadle's lips; he has the proper pride of an artist.] But Tom tells me not to be frightened, for he's only a-shammin'. Then the peeler tells us to move on, and you comes up and gives Tom a shillin'; and the first thing Tom does is to buy a poloney for me and a 'unk o' bread for the tiger.

Tom Beadle. I wish I may die, sir, if she ain't told the truth, the 'ole truth, and nothin' but the truth, so 'elp me Bob!

Blade-o'-Grass gazes at Mr. Merrywhistle eagerly, and with glistening eyes, and seeing that her vindication of Tom has raised him in the estimation of their benefactor, nods at her ragged companion two or three times in satisfaction. Mr. Merrywhistle, in his heart of hearts, forgives Tom for the deception--nay, finds justification for it; and the children are allowed to depart with their spoil.

Mr. Merrywhistle. That's a sad sight, and a sad tale.

Robert Truefit. England's full of such sights and such tales.

Jimmy Virtue pricked up his ears. He knew when his friend Bob was 'coming out,' and he prepared himself to listen by taking out his glass eye and contemplating it with his fierce eye, polishing it up the while.

Mr. Merrywhistle [gently]. Not full of such sights, surely?

Robert Truefit. Yes, full of them, unfortunately. Take London. There are thousands and thousands of such children in such positions as Tom Beadle and Blade-o'-Grass, hanging about the courts and alleys--pushed out of sight, one might almost say. And as London is, so every other large English city is. If they haven't shoals of boys and girls growing up to men and women in one bad way, they have them in another bad way. I know what old Jimmy got me here for to-day--he wanted me to talk; he knows I'm fond of it.

Jimmy Virtue. Bob ought to be in Parleyment. He'd tell 'em somethin'.

Robert Truefit. That's a specimen of old Jimmy's flattery, sir. I don't see what good I could do in Parliament. I've got to work for my living, and that takes up all my time; if I were in Parliament, I should have to get money somehow to support my wife and family, and it isn't in my blood to become a pensioner. Besides, I should be contented enough with what's called 'the ruling powers,' if they'd only turn their attention more to such social questions as this.

Mr. Merrywhistle. Ah, I'm glad of that; I'm glad you're not a republican.

Robert Truefit. Not I, sir--though I don't know what I might become by and by; for there's no denying that things are unequal, and that working men are talking of this inequality more and more every year. You'd be surprised to know what they think about this and that. And although I don't go so far as some of them do, I can't help agreeing with them in many things.

Mr. Merrywhistle. But what do they want? Equality? Such a thing is impossible.

Robert Truefit. I know it is. You'd have to do away with brains before you got that; though there are a many who believe that it is to be arrived at. Some of them are fools, and some of them are rogues; but some of them have really worked themselves up into absolute belief.

Mr. Merrywhistle. Discontented people are to be found everywhere, and under any form of government.

Robert Truefit. Ay, that's the way a great many sum up; when they say that, they think they have found out the cause, and that the matter is settled. 'Tisn't the sensible way to view it.

Mr. Merrywhistle. What is the reason, then, of this spread of feeling among working-men?

Robert Truefit. That's a large question, and would take too long to answer. But I think the penny newspaper is partly accountable for it. They can afford to buy the penny and halfpenny newspaper, and they read them, and talk more among themselves. You see, things press upon them. They are arriving at a sort of belief that the laws are made more for the protection and benefit of property than for the protection and benefit of flesh and blood; and as their value in the market doesn't lie in land and money, but in bone and muscle, the idea isn't pleasant to them.

Mr. Merrywhistle. But surely they are not right in this idea?

Robert Truefit. Are they not? Read the newspapers, and you'll find they are. Why, a man may do anything to flesh and blood, short of murder, and the law won't be very hard on him. But let him touch property, ever so little, and down it comes on him like a sledge-hammer. I'll tell you what I read in the police reports this morning. A man is had up at the police-court for beating his wife. The woman is put into the box, with marks on her face and with her head bandaged; the man doesn't deny that he beat her, and half-a-dozen witnesses prove that he beat her cruelly; the floor of the room in which they lived was covered with blood-stains. There is no excuse for him; no aggravation on her part is set up; a doctor states, that if one of the blows she received had been a little more on the left of her head, she would have been killed; and the man gets three months' hard labour. Afterwards, a man is brought up for stealing three-and-sixpence. He is miserably dressed, and there is want in his face. The evidence in this case is quite as clear as in the other. The prisoner snatched a purse, containing three-and-sixpence, out of a man's hand, and ran away. Being searched, not a farthing is found upon him, nor anything of the value of a farthing. The man does not deny the theft, and says he wanted a meal; the police know nothing of him; and he gets three months' hard labour. Compare these equal sentences with the unequal offences, and you will see the relative value of property and human flesh in the criminal market.

Jimmy Virtue. Bob puts it plainly, doesn't he?

Mr. Merrywhistle. But these cases must be rare.

Robert Truefit. They are very common; and these two cases that I have put side by side, are two of the mildest. Listen to this--another wife-beating case: Husband comes home at noon. What kind of man he is may be guessed from his first words to his wife: 'I've something to tell thee, you----! I'm going to murder thee, you----!' He takes off his jacket, calls his bulldog, and sets it at his wife. As the dog flies at the woman, her husband hits her in the face; the dog drags her from the sofa, with its teeth in her flesh (it is almost too horrible to tell, but it is true, every word of it), and the husband jumps upon her, and kicks her on the head and shoulders. Imploring him to have mercy upon her, crying for help, the woman is dragged by the dog from room to room, tearing flesh out of her. The frightful struggle continues for some time, until the woman manages to make her escape from the house. It is dreadful to read the doctor's description of the state of the woman, and how he feared, for three or four days, that mortification would set in. The man is sentenced to--what do you think? Six months' hard labour. About the same time, a very young man is found guilty of stealing twenty shillings' worth of metal, and he gets seven years' penal servitude. But I could multiply these instances. You may say, that such cases as these have nothing to do with the broad question of misgovernment; but I maintain that they have. You get your criminal material from such places as Stoney-alley, where poor Blade-o'-Grass lives; and yet Stoney-alley is as bad now--ay, and worse than it was fifty years ago. The law knows of its existence, has its wakeful eye upon it; but what has the law done for its good, or for the good of those who live there? Take the case of Blade-o'-Grass. What does the law do for her?--and by the law you must understand that I mean the governing machinery for keeping society in order and for dispensing justice to all--out of our police-courts as well as in them. Think of the story she told, and the way in which she told it. There is capacity for good, in that child--ay, and in Tom Beadle, too. Can you doubt that, but for your charity, she might have died of hunger?

Mr. Merrywhistle [eagerly]. Then you don't disapprove of indiscriminate charity?

Robert Truefit. Not I; I don't disapprove of a man putting his hand into his pocket and exercising a benevolent impulse. Your lip-philanthropists, who preach against indiscriminate charity--what would they do for Blade-o'-Grass? What would they do! What do they do? 'Work,' they say. But they don't? give her work; don't even teach her how to work, if such a miracle happened to fall in her way. And all the while the policeman says, 'Move on.' I know something, through Jimmy here, of Blade-o'-Grass--a hapless waif, an encumbrance, a blot, serving as a theme for countless meetings and oceans of words. What business has she in the world? But she came, unfortunately for herself, and she is so legislated for, that to live is her greatest affliction.

Jimmy Virtue. It's my opinion that a good many of the fellers who preach agin indiscriminate charity only do so as an excuse for buttonin' up their pockets.

Robert Truefit [laughing]. And their hearts as well, Jimmy. You put me in mind of something I saw last Sunday in Upper-street, Islington. The people were coming out of church. A couple--evidently man and wife-were walking before me, talking on religious matters--or, rather, he was talking, and she was listening. I passed them just as he was saying, 'If I haven't got the grace of God in my heart, I'd like to know who has got it?' and at the same moment as forlorn-looking a woman as ever I set eyes on, intercepted him, and curtseyed, and held out her hand imploringly. He pushed her aside surlily and with a sour look on his face; and walked along talking of the grace of God. The woman may have been an impostor--in other words, a professional beggar; but I should be sorry to call that Grace-of-God man my friend. No, sir, I don't think that it is a good thing to crush a kindly impulse, or that we should treat our best feelings and emotions as so many figures in a sum. It is not the giver who makes beggars. The fault is in the system, which opens no road for them at the proper time of their lives.

Mr. Merrywhistle [sadly]. But tell me: do you see no remedy for these ills?

Robert Truefit. The remedy is simple. Commence at the right end. Train up a child in the way it should go, and when it is old it will not depart from it. And by the same rule, Train up a child in the way it shouldn't go, and when it is old it will not depart from it. It is almost time for me and Jimmy to be off. Jimmy wants to open his shop, and I want to get home to my wife; but I'll just try to explain what I mean. Two poor boys, one six and one nine years of age, lost their mother; a few weeks afterwards they were caught taking some potatoes from a garden. The presumption is, that they were hungry. The potatoes were valued at one penny. The boys were sent to prison for fourteen days, and the State thus commenced their education. I will conclude with a personal experience. I had occasion to go to Liverpool some little time ago, and on the day that I was to return to London I saw a girl standing against a wall, crying bitterly. She was a pretty girl, of about sixteen years of age. I went and spoke to her, and soon saw that the poor girl was utterly bewildered. It appeared that she had landed that morning in Liverpool, having been brought by her sister from Ireland, and that her sister had deserted her. A more simple, artless girl I never met, and she hadn't a penny in her pocket, nor a friend in the Liverpool wilderness. I thought to myself. This girl will come to harm. Hungry, friendless, pretty---- I went to a policeman, and told him the story. The policeman scratched his head. 'Is she a bad girl?' he asked. I was shocked at the question, and said no, I was sure she was not; that she was a simple good girl, almost a child--and was as complete an outcast as if she were among savages. The policeman shrugged his shoulders, and said civilly enough that he couldn't do anything. 'What did you mean by asking if she was a bad girl?' I asked. 'Well, you see,' he answered, 'if she was a bad girl, and wanted to be took care of, I could take her somewhere.' 'Where she would be taken care of?' I asked. 'Yes,' he answered. 'And have food given to her? 'Yes.' 'But a good girl,' I said, 'homeless, friendless, and hungry----"Can't interfere with them,' said the policeman. 'She'll have to qualify herself for a refuge, then,' I could not help saying bitterly, as I turned away, leaving the poor girl in her distress; for I could do nothing, and had only enough money to take me third-class to London. There, sir! You can draw your own moral from these things. Many a working man is drawing conclusions from suchlike circumstances, and the feeling that statesmen are ignoring the most important problems of the day is gaining strength rapidly. For my own part, I honestly confess that, without one tinge of socialism or even republicanism in my veins, I am not satisfied with things as they are.

With these words, spoken very earnestly, Robert Truefit, accompanied by Jimmy Virtue, took his departure. But Jimmy Virtue found time to whisper in Mr. Merrywhistle's ear,

'Didn't I tell you Bob 'ud talk to you? It ain't dear at sixpence an hour, is it?

Mr. Merrywhistle said no; it was not at all dear, and he hoped soon to see them again.

'All right,' said Jimmy Virtue, with a last flash from his fierce eye; 'when you like;' and so departed.

THE INTERLUDE.

In times gone by, it used to be the sometime fashion in the theatres to have an interlude between the acts of the melodrama, so that the mind might find some relief from the thrilling horrors which had just been enacted, and might prepare itself for the more profound horrors to come. Usually, there was an interval of time between the acts--in most cases seven years--during which the performers neither changed their linen nor grew any older. This was probably owing to the joyous efforts of those who enacted the interlude, which was invariably composed of songs and dances. Of such material as these shall part of this interlude be composed; striking out the songs, however, and introducing flowers in their stead, as being infinitely more innocent and graceful than the gross and impure lessons taught by the popular songs of the day, which unfortunately flow too readily into such neighbourhoods as that of which Stoney-alley forms a limb. Such teaching, in its own sad time, will bear bitter fruit--nay, it is bearing it even now, and the poisoned branches are bending beneath the weight.

Blade-o'-Grass was very young; but the few years she had lived contained many imminent crises--any one of which, but for some timely act of human kindness, might have put an end to her existence. But her life had not been all shade, although it may appear to you and me to have been so; there were lights in it, there were times when she enjoyed. You and I stand in the sun, and contemplate with sadness our fellow-creatures struggling and living in the dark. But it is not dark to them, as it is to us; they were born in it, they live in it, they are used to it. Such sunlight as we enjoy, and are, I hope, thankful for, might make them drunk.

Said Tom Beadle one day to Blade-o'-Grass,

'I say, Bladergrass, why don't yer do somethin', and make a few coppers?'

And Blade-o'-Grass very naturally answered,

'What shall I do, Tom?'

Tom was prepared with his answer.

'Lookee 'ere: why don't you be a flower-gal?'

'O, Tom!' exclaimed Blade-o'-Grass, her face flushing, her heart beating, at the prospect of heaven held out to her. 'A flower-gal, Tom! A flower-gal! O, don't I wish I could be!'

'You'd 'ave to wash yer face, yer know,' said Tom, regarding the dirty face of Blade-o'-Grass from a business point of view, 'and put a clean frock on.'

Down to zero went the hopes of Blade-o'-Grass. A clean face she might have compassed. But a clean frock! That meant a new frock, of course. Blade-o'-Grass had never had a new frock in her life. A new frock! She had never had anything new--not even a new bootlace. Despair was in her face. Tom saw it, and said,

'Don't be down in the mug, Bladergrass. We'll see if it can't be done some'ow.'

What a hero Tom was in her eyes!

'O, Tom,' she cried, 'if I could be a flower-gal--if I could! I've seen 'em at the Royal Igschange'--she was pretty well acquainted with that locality by this time--'and don't they look prime!' She twined her fingers together nervously. 'They've all got clean faces and nice dresses. O, 'ow 'appy they must be!'

'And they make lots o' money,' said Tom.

'Do they! O, don't I wish I was them!'

'And they go to theaytres.'

'Do they! O, don't I wish I could go to the theaytre!'

'There's Poll Buttons. Why, two year ago, Bladergrass, she was raggeder nor you. And now she comes out--she does come out, I can tell yer! She sells flowers at the Royal Igschange, and she looks as 'appy'--as 'appy'--Tom's figures of speech and similes were invariably failures--'as 'appy as can be. Why, I see her the other night at the Standard, and she was in the pit. There was a feller with her a-suckin' a stick. Didn't she look proud! And I 'eerd Bill Britton say as how he saw her at 'Ighbury Barn last Sunday with another feller a-suckin' a stick.'

'Do all the swells suck sticks, Tom?' asked Blade-o'-Grass innocently.

'All the real tip-toppers do,' answered Tom.

'Perhaps there's somethin' nice in the knobs,' suggested Blade-o'-Grass.

'Perhaps; but I don't think it. You see, it looks swellish, Bladergrass.'

'If you 'ad a stick, would you suck it, Tom?'

'I think I should,' replied Tom, after a little consideration; 'and I'd 'ave one with a large knob. They're all the go.' Then Tom came back to the subject of Poll Buttons. 'She makes a 'eap o' money. Why, I 'eerd tell as 'ow she sells crocuses and wilets for a tanner a bunch at first. The swells buy a bunch of wilets, and then she coaxes 'em, and ses as 'ow wilets and crocuses ought to go together, and she uses 'er eyes and smiles sweet. Stand up, Bladergrass!'

Blade-o'-Grass stood up, and Tom Beadle scrutinised her.

'Poll Buttons is a reg'lar beauty, they say. But I wish I may die if you won't be a reg'larer beauty when you're as old as Poll is.'

'Shall I, Tom? Shall I?' And the eyes of Blade-o'-Grass sparkled, and a bright colour came into her cheeks. Even in her ragged frock, and with her dirty face, she looked pretty. 'Then I shall get a tanner a bunch for my crocuses and wilets, and when the roses comes in, I'll--I'll----' But her voice trailed off as she looked at her ragged frock, and her lips trembled, and the little glimpse of heaven that lay in the imaginary basket of flowers faded utterly away.

'Don't take on so, Bladergrass,' said Tom Beadle; 'who knows? I may 'ave a bit o' luck. And if I do, I wish I may die if I don't set you up as a flower-gal! You jist keep up your 'art, and wait a bit.'

And one day Tom Beadle really went to Jimmy Virtue's leaving-shop, and asked the price of a new cotton frock, which, after much bargaining, he bought for two shillings and fourpence.

'Who's it for, Tom?' asked Jimmy, testing the coins before he delivered the frock to Tom. 'Got a new sweet'art?'

'It's for Bladergrass,' replied Tom complacently. 'I'm a-goin' to set her up as a flower-gal. I promised 'er I would when I 'ad a bit o' luck.'

'And you've 'ad a bit o' luck?'

'Yes, a reg'lar slice.'

'How was it, Tom?'

'Arks no questions, and I'll tell 'you no lies,' responded Tom saucily, walking away with his precious purchase.

Neither will we be too curious about how the means were acquired which enabled Tom to give Blade-o'-Grass an honest start in life.

That first new common cotton dress! What joy and delight stirred the heart of Blade-o'-Grass as she surveyed it! She devoured it with her eyes, and was as delicate in handling it as if its texture had been of the finest silk. All that she could say was, 'O, Tom! O, Tom!' She threw her arms round Tom's neck, and kissed him a hundred times; and Tom felt how sweet it is to give. But Tom's goodness did not end here. He conducted Blade-o'-Grass to a room where she could wash herself and array herself in her new dress. She came out of that room transformed. She had smoothed her hair and washed her face, and the dress became her. She smiled gratefully at Tom when she presented herself to him.

'I'm blessed if Poll Buttons'll be able to 'old a candle to you!' exclaimed Tom admiringly, and Blade-o'-Grass thrilled with joy.

Thus it came about that Mr. Merrywhistle, walking near the Royal Exchange one day, saw a clean little girl, with a basket of humble flowers on her arm, and a bright little face looking earnestly at him.

'Bless my soul!' exclaimed the benevolent gentleman. 'Blade-o'-Grass!'

'Yes, sir, if you please. Tom's set me up as a flower-gal.'

'Tom!'

'Tom Beadle, sir; 'im as you guv a shillin' to once, and as come along o' me when we 'ad that jolly dinner.'

'Dear me! Dear me!' said Mr. Merrywhistle, honest pleasure beaming in his eyes. 'And Tom's set you up, eh? And you're getting an honest living, eh?'

'Yes, sir, if you please, sir. Do you want a flower for your button'ole, sir? 'Ere's a white rose, sir--a reg'lar beauty; and 'ere's a piece o' mingyonet to show it off, sir, and a bit o' maiden 'air to back it up.'

And before Mr. Merrywhistle knew where he was, he had put the flowers in his button-hole, and, instructed by Blade-o'-Grass, had fastened them with a pin she took out of her frock. It was thirty years since he had worn a flower, the good old fellow! and as he looked upon them now, there came to him the memory of a few sunny months when he was young. The crowds of people, the busy streets, the noise and turmoil, vanished from sight and sense; and for one brief moment--which might have been an hour, the vision was so distinct--he saw fair fingers fastening a piece of mignonette in his coat, and a fair head bending to his breast---- It was gone! But as Mr. Merrywhistle awoke to the busy hum about him, there was a sweet breath in his nostrils, and a dim sweet light in his eyes. Most unwisely he gave Blade-o'-Grass a shilling for the flowers, and patted her head, and walked away; while Blade-o'-Grass herself, almost fearing that the shilling was a bad one, bit it with her strong teeth, and being satisfied of its genuineness, executed a double-shuffle on the kerbstone.

That very afternoon, Blade-o'-Grass, having had a good day, purchased a walking cane of a street vendor. It was a cane with the largest knob he had in his stock. This cane she presented to Tom Beadle the same evening. Tom was immensely delighted with it. To the admiration of Blade-o'-Grass, he put the knob in his mouth, to the serious danger of that feature, and comported himself as became a tip-top swell.

'You're a reg'lar little brick,' said Tom; 'and I'm blessed if I don't take you to the theaytre.'

Blade-o'-Grass jumped for joy and clapped her hands. How she had longed to go to a theatre! And now the magic hour had come. She had been rich enough lately to pay twopence a night for a bed, and she went to the cheap lodging-house she patronised, and washed her face and combed her hair, and made herself as smart as she could. Tom Beadle had also smartened himself up, and to the theatre they went, arm in arm, he with the knob of the stick in his mouth, and she, in her rags, as proud as any peacock.

In what words can the awe and wonder of Blade-o'-Grass be described? She had her own ideas of things, and she was surprised to find the interior of the theatre so different from what she had imagined. Boxes, pit, and gallery, she knew there were. But she had set down in her mind that the boxes were veritable boxes, in which the people were shut, with little eye-holes to peep through; and the pit she had imagined as a large dark space dug out of the earth, very low down, where the people were all huddled together, and had to look up to see what was going on. It was to the pit they went, and for some time Blade-o'-Grass was too astonished to speak. A very, very large O would fitly describe her condition. Tom Beadle, on the contrary, was quite composed; theatres were but ordinary places to him. But used-up as he was to the pleasures of the town, he derived a new pleasure from the contemplation of the wonderment of Blade-o'-Grass.

'O, Tom! O, Tom!' she whispered in ecstasy, edging closer to him, when at last she found courage to use her tongue. It was a large theatre, with a great deal of gold-leaf about it; and the audience were evidently bent upon enjoying themselves, and vehemently applauded at every possible opportunity. Thus, when the lights are turned up, and a bright blaze breaks out upon the living sea of faces, there is much clapping of hands, and much stamping of feet, and other marks of approval. When the musicians straggle into the orchestra, they are also vehemently applauded; but those 'high and mighty' might have been by themselves in the Desert of Sahara, for all the heed they pay to the audience. The occupiers of the gallery are very noisy in their demonstrations, and issue their commands with stentorian lungs. 'Now, then; scrape up, cat-gut!' 'Hoo-o-o-o! Scrape up! Up with the rag!' with cries, and shouts, and whistles, which strike fresh wonderment to the soul of Blade-o'-Grass. She is not frightened at the noise; for even Tom Beadle puts his two little fingers to the corners of his lips, and adds shrill whistles to the general confusion--in the performance of which duty he stretches his mouth to such an extent that, as a feature, it becomes a hideous mockery. But at length the band strikes up with a crash, the sound of which is speedily drowned in the roar of delight that follows. In due time--but not in time to satisfy the impatient audience--the music ceases, and a general shifting and rustling takes place among the audience. A moments breathless expectation follows; a cracked bell gives the meanest of tinkles; and Blade-o'-Grass bends a little more forward as that awful and magic green curtain is drawn upwards by invisible hands. The piece that is there and then represented to the wondering soul of Blade-o'-Grass is a 'strong domestic drama,' as the playbill has it, and Blade-o'-Grass gasps and sobs and catches her breath at the 'striking' situations with which the play is filled. The piece is a narration of the struggles and vicissitudes of the poorest class of the community--the class indeed, the lower stratum of which is occupied by just such persons as Tom Beadle and Blade-o'-Grass; and a curious commentary is made on it the next day by Blade-o'-Grass, who, dilating upon its wonders and entrancements, declares that she 'never seed sich a thing in all her born days.' There are of course in the piece a painfully-virtuous wife, a desperate villain, to whom murder is child's play, a delirium-tremens beggar, a Good Young Man, and a vilified Jew; and as these characters play their parts, Blade-o'-Grass thrills and quivers with delicious excitement. Tom Beadle also enters into the excitement of the representation, and stamps and claps his hands and whistles as vigorously as any one there. But when the 'strong domestic drama' is concluded, and the glories of the burlesque are unfolded to the ravished senses of Blade-o'-Grass, then, indeed, is she in heaven. Never has she conceived anything so enchanting as this. It is the first fairy story that has ever been presented to her. How she screams over the meaningless songs! How she devours with her eyes the display of female limbs! 'O, 'ow lovely, Tom!' she whispers. 'O, don't I wish I was them!'

'You'd look as well as any of 'em, Bladergrass,' says Tom, who knows everything, 'if you was took in 'and, and if you could darnce.'

'O no, Tom--O no!' exclaims Blade-o'-Grass: 'I ain't got sich legs.'

Tom laughs, and whispers confidentially that 'them legs ain't all their own. He knows a cove who knows a balley-gal, and she pads her legs like one o'clock.' Blade-o'-Grass, in her heart of hearts, can't believe it; but she is too much absorbed in the performance to enter into argument. So the ant passes before her eyes until all the songs are sung and all the dances danced; and when the curtain falls upon the brilliant last scene, she looks solemnly at Tom, and a great sob escapes her because it is all over. She can scarcely repress her tears. It is a wondrous night for Blade-o'-Grass, and lives in her memory for long afterwards. Tom Beadle proposes 'a eel supper,' and they sit in state, like the best nobles in the land, in a dirty box in a dirty eel-pie shop; and as they eat their eels off a dirty plate, with a dirty spoon and fork, Blade-o'-Grass looks up to her companion as to a god; and Tom, noticing the girl's sparkling eyes and flushed cheeks, says, with an approving nod, 'I'm blessed if you won't beat Poll Buttons into fits.' Then they go home, and Blade-o'-Grass dreams that she is an angel hanging from the flies.

That first night at a theatre filled Blade-o'-Grass with a new ambition, and her better prospects inspired her with confidence. She determined to learn to dance.

You will, I am sure, be amazed to hear, that every night in Stoney-alley, when the weather was in any way propitious, there was a ball--an open-air ball; the orchestra, an Italian organ-grinder; the company, nearly all the dirty boys and girls in the neighbourhood. At a certain hour every evening an Italian organ-grinder, on whose dark face a fixed expression of stolid gloomy melancholy for ever rested, made his appearance in Stoney-alley; and, as if he were a lost soul, and this agony was his penance, ground out of his afflicted organ a string of waltzes and polkas and quadrilles, so inexpressibly dismal that the very dogs howled in despair, and fled. But directly the first note sounded--and that first note always came out with a wail--the children, from two years old and upwards, began to congregate, and without any curtseying, or bowing, or engaging of partners, the strangest ball commenced that ever was seen.

Girls with babies in their arms glided round and round in the entrancing waltz; children who could scarcely toddle toddled round; and young ladies without encumbrances clasped each other by the waist, and spun round in a state of beatific bliss. When the waltz music ended with a groan, and the polka commenced with a wheeze, the big children hopped and the toddlers toddled in perfect contentment. Then came the quadrilles, in which many new figures were introduced, which Belgravia might have profited by. But the strangest dance of all was a Scotch reel, which, by some unearthly means, had got into this decrepit organ, and which, being set to work by the inexorable handle, came out of its hiding-place spasmodically, and with stitches in its side. It was a sight to remember to see these ragged children dance this Scotch reel, with their toes up to their knees, their right arms elevated above their heads, and their left hands stuck in their sides as if they grew there. Blade-o'-Grass had never had courage to join in the revels; she had been too ragged and forlorn to claim equality with even this ragged and forlorn troop. But now her prospects were brightening, and her ambition was roused. The very evening following that on which she visited the theatre she boldly joined the dancers. And there she hopped and twirled and glided until the music ceased; and every evening thereafter she made her appearance at the entertainment as punctually as some people attend their places of worship, and with more devotion than many. She was looked upon as a guest of high distinction at the ball, for she was liberal with her farthings and halfpence. In course of time she became one of the very best dancers in the alley, and often and often dreamt that she was a ballet-girl, and was twirling before an admiring audience, in the shortest of short spangled skirts, and the pinkest of pink legs.

These were the happiest days she had ever known. Now and then the tiger set up its claims, and was not satisfied; but these occasions were very rare. She went to the theatre often, and sometimes treated Tom Beadle, who did not show a stupid pride and independence. She sold flowers in the season, and lived how she could when there were no flowers to sell. 'I wish they growed all the yeer round,' she said to Tom many and many a time. She and Tom were always together, and it was understood that they had 'taken up with one another.'

This being an interlude, in which the promise set forth has been faithfully carried out-- for dances and flowers have been introduced in profusion--it will perhaps be considered out of place to mention that, excepting that she knew how to speak an intelligible language, Blade-o'-Grass was as ignorant of morals and religion as if she had been a four-footed animal. But it is necessary to state this, or you might condemn her unjustly, and look down upon her uncharitably. And while she grew in deeper and deeper ignorance, how the great world laboured, in which she lived and moved and had her being! One section was in agony because a man of science had by his writings thrown doubt on the grand story of the Creation, and had attempted to prove that Adam and Eve were not created; and nine-tenths of the people shrunk in horror from a man who denied the truth of biblical miracles. Yet one and all believed in a future state--a better one than this, a higher one than this, a holier one than this--to be earned by living a good life, and by doing unto others as we would others should do unto us. And Blade-o'-Grass had never raised her eyes and hands to God; she had never said a prayer.

www.ingramcontent.com/pod-product-compliance
Lightning Source LLC
LaVergne TN
LVHW081545060526
838200LV00048B/2214